C000177316

THE
CHARITY
SHOPS
HANDBOOK

HILARY BLUME

A Charities Advisory Trust Publication

THE CHARITY SHOPS HANDBOOK

by Hilary Blume

Published by the Charities Advisory Trust,
Radius Works, Back Lane, London NW3 1HL

© 1995 The Charities Advisory Trust

No part of this publication may be reproduced in any form whatsoever without prior written permission from the publisher.

Charities Advisory Trust is registered charity no. 1040487

Designed and typeset by Andrew Westoby

Printed and bound by W M Print Limited, Walsall

Thanks to the following publishers who gave permission to reproduce from their publications: '

Corporate Intelligence Research Publications Ltd
Scriptographic Publications Limited
Charities Aid Foundation
NGO Finance

British Library Cataloguing in Publication Data
A catalogue record for this book is available from the British Library

ISBN 1 873860 77 3

ACKNOWLEDGEMENTS

Lots of people have helped me write this book. Members of the Charity Shops Group - Joyce Brattan, David Harker, Alan Greener, Linda Esesien, Adrian Barker and John Tough have been generous in sharing information, as has Colin Sandford and Hugh Belshaw.

Andrew Westoby has been unfailingly courteous and helpful in preparing the manuscript, although my vagueness and constant alterations must have been very trying. Mark Pountney has helped research the statistics, and showed both doggedness and numeracy, wonderful qualities for a researcher. Bob Holman, a trustee of the Charities Advisory Trust, the only person who ever dared tell me it was time I finished the book, also earns my gratitude.

Above all I should thank Lekha Klouda, my friend and colleague at the Charities Advisory Trust, who has taken on the burden of a great deal of work, which enabled me to find time in which to write this book.

Hilary Blume

ACKNOWLEDGEMENTS

CONTENTS

INTRODUCTION

Charity shops are primarily a British institution. Although there are "Goodwill Stores" in America selling donated and hand-made goods, there are many fewer than in the UK, where Oxfam is amongst the top ten retailers, measured by number of outlets. In the Irish Republic charity shops are a well-established means of fund-raising, but in the rest of Europe there are few charity shops, and those are often the initiative of a British exile.

Fair trade shops, selling goods from projects in the Third World, are more usual, particularly in Northern Europe and Scandinavia. For sheer scale of enterprise the UK is the world leader in charity shops.

There has been a market for second hand clothes for centuries, and the second hand clothes dealer is the stuff of many Dickens novels. By the end of the 19th century both the second hand clothes shop and the charity jumble sale offered a large selection of used clothing to the urban poor. The rise of cheap, manufactured, ready to wear clothing may have widened the choice, but demand for second hand clothing continued. The rag and bone man, driving round in a horse and cart, collecting discarded household items, in exchange for plants, or trinkets, or gold fish, persisted right into the 1960s. Whilst most of the textiles went for 'shoddy', the better quality items of discarded clothing would be sold through second hand shops.

For the last fifty years the number of commercial second hand clothes shops has declined and the number of charity shops has mushroomed. The ubiquitous jumble sale has become somewhat overtaken by the car boot sale, where the sponsoring organisation, often a charity, has income from rents and transfers the trouble of acquiring and selling stock to the pitch holders.

'CHARITY SHOP' AS DEFINED IN THIS BOOK MEANS ...

- a shop selling mainly donated goods
- whose profits are used for charitable purpose
- which is normally operated by a charity

THE SIZE OF THE CHARITY SHOP SECTOR

- estimated 5,500 charity shops throughout the UK
- estimated annual turnover £200 million
- this represents 0.2% of national retail sales

There are now thought to be around five and a half thousand charity shops selling donated goods, throughout the UK. Oxfam, the clear market leader, has developed from two shops in 1960 to around 850 in the mid 1990s. Charities have been establishing charity shops at an increasing rate. Entering later into the field than Oxfam, the rate of development has often been very rapid. For example, the Imperial Cancer Research Fund have expanded their shop chain from 245 in 1989 to 470 in 1993; the Cancer Research Campaign from 50 to 211 shops and British Heart Foundation from 34 to 194 shops in the same period.

CHARITY SHOPS: LARGEST CHAINS 1994

NAME OF CHARITY	NO. OF SHOPS	RANK OF THE CHARITY BY SIZE OF TOTAL INCOME
Oxfam	842	2
Imperial Cancer Research Fund	470	5
Sue Ryder Foundation	460	36
Barnardos	307	7
British Red Cross	306	15
Spastics Society	250	19
Help the Aged	243	8
Cancer Research Campaign	211	6
Age Concern	210	49
British Heart Foundation	194	14

Figures from Dimensions of the Voluntary Sector (CAF) Pub. Jan 1995

Charity shops used to be temporary, fleeting affairs - occupying unlet shops or fag ends of leases. Now the majority are not only permanent, some indeed occupying freeholds, but also in prime trading positions, particularly in high streets in country and market towns.

The recession has also made it possible for many charities to be offered prime shops, for which the landlords cannot find tenants. There are now charity shops within yards of Oxford Street!

If the development plans of the larger charities are realised and smaller charities continue to open shops locally, then the number of charity shops may reach between eight and ten thousand by the end of the century. The hospice movement are particularly strong in the sector, both by the profitability of their shops and the rate of expansion. Though one must consider that were the increase to be so dramatic the profitability of the shops might decline, and the attractions of expansion evaporate.

Why do charities want to set up charity shops, and why do they appear to want to expand the size of their chains? Nearly all those running shops identify three main reasons

- firstly, to raise funds for the charity;
- secondly, to promote awareness of the charity;
- thirdly, because charity shops are an acceptable way of fund raising.

Most charity shops run at a profit. Cumulatively this may be very substantial. In financial year 1992-3 Oxfam's profit from its charity shops was nearly £19m, Imperial Cancer Research Fund over £6.5m, Spastics Society (SCOPE) £4.5m. These are substantial amounts, so it is no wonder that other players are tempted to join in. (For full figures on the turnover and profits of the largest chains or charity shops. See chapter 7).

- the charity shop is a permanent billboard promoting the charity's name

- it is a convenient collection point for donations

Not only is it possible to raise substantial money through charity shops, but it has the virtue of being a relatively dependable and regular source of funds. It does not depend on any particular appeal, and is not likely to vary greatly or be much affected by uncontrollable external factors. A major economic recession may reduce the quality and quantity of donated goods, and lead to a fall in sales, but it will probably have less affect on shop profits than on other forms of fund-raising.

Charities have come to depend on income from their shops with a confidence that they do not have in other funding sources. For charities, shops income can represent their core income. Not only is the income from shops a relatively dependable source, it also has the advantage to the charity that it is not tied to any project, it is unconditional. Many charities find it hard to fund-raise for their general work (including administrative costs). Funds may come in as a result of a particular appeal for famine relief, or to build a new hospice, or support a particular residential home but generating the day to day running costs is more difficult.

Money given to a charity for a specific purpose must be used for that purpose. Money given for the general purposes of the charity, as is the income from shops, can be used by the charity as needed. If the charity can rely on a certain level of income from its shops, even when it is being prudent in calculating the level of profit, it can plan for the future with some confidence.

The presence of a charity shop, with the name of the charity on its fascia board, provides a permanent reminder of the charity and its cause, and as such provides a permanent appeal for funds. Having a chain of charity shops is part of a campaign to increase public awareness of a charity's existence. Usually the name of the charity is sufficient to highlight its cause (for example, Imperial Cancer Research Fund, Help the Aged, Save the Children Fund tell you within the name what the broad area of their work is) and the presence of the name in a busy shopping street reminds passers-by of the need. This is important as an appeal for funds, not only legacies, but also one-off donations.

Most charity shops will receive cash donations from passers-by, not just from customers putting their change into a collecting box, but people who will come in and make a donation, either stimulated by a television programme, or news report, or because of a personal experience, such as the death of a relative or a happy event like the birth of a child. The shop is a well placed collecting box. If people are familiar with the name of the charity, and the shop is a permanent billboard site, the charity's fund raising task is much easier.

Charities relying on legacies as a source of income, or for those hoping to attract a large number of legacies, it is very important to keep the charity's name in the public limelight, because people making their wills, other than those who are known to the charity and nurtured by them, will put in as beneficiaries charities they know the name of. They may need prompting by their solicitors, or they may know the name because they see it daily on the way to and from the shops. Generally people do not carry out research into which charity or charities they name in their wills. Considering the amounts of money involved they are surprisingly casual. (Perhaps it is a tribute to what is seen as the general efficacy of the charitable sector as a whole that testators feel their money will be well spent by virtually any charity).

Of course, if the name of the charity is associated with a dirty, badly run shop then the fund-raising task is made harder, but in general terms, all charities see the promotion of the name of the charity as an important advantage of having a chain of charity shops.

At a time when various fund raising methods are held in public opprobrium, charity shops selling donated goods are seen as a socially useful form of fund-raising. Generally, members of the public believe charity shops are a good thing. Surveys show that whilst not everyone would buy from a charity shop there is virtually universal approval in principle to donating goods to charity shops. Charity shops are seen as socially desirable, not only because they provide a source of cheap goods for those who are on low incomes, but also because through re-cycling it makes good use of resources.

It is sometimes wrongly assumed that those whom the charity shop is supposed to benefit is the poor customer. In fact the benefit is supposed to be for the charity which is generating income. Thus a Cancer Research Campaign shop is intended to raise funds for cancer research, Age Concern shops for the elderly. Social service to the poor and the re-cycling of unwanted goods, are positive benefits from charity shops to the community but they are not what motivates the charities to set them up. Interestingly, it has not been the charities established to protect the environment, or save the earth's resources, which have set up chains of thrift shops.

THREE MAIN REASONS FOR CHARITIES OPENING SHOPS

- raise funds
- increase awareness
- popular with donors

1

CHARITY LAW, TAX & VAT

Rules for charity shops

Tax concessions

When a trading company is needed

Primary purpose trading

Rate relief

Charity shops should be run by the charity

Protection of the charity's reputation

Problems of investing in a subsidiary company

Capital gains tax

Are shops run by a trading subsidiary better managed

Closing down a trading company

Limiting trustees' liability

Value Added Tax

CHARITY LAW, TAX AND VAT RULES FOR CHARITY SHOPS

Charity shops are given substantial tax concessions because all the profits are used to further the charity's work, which is perceived as of public benefit. Any shopkeeper who gave all the profits of his business to charity could arrange it so that these funds were for the most part also tax exempt. The reasons for the concessions are not that the shop is run by a charity, but that all profit is applied for charitable purpose. Because there are substantial concessions, safeguards are needed to stop companies masquerading as charities for tax avoidance purposes.

TAX CONCESSIONS FOR CHARITY SHOPS

- exempt corporation tax on profits
- 80% mandatory rate relief and possible 20% discretionary rate relief
- zero VAT rating

The Charity Commission, the Inland Revenue and Customs and Excise all have regulatory roles in monitoring the probity of charities. The Charity Commission is primarily involved at the point of registration, although they do some spot check monitoring, to see that charities are doing what they are supposed to do. The Inland Revenue will scrutinise annual accounts particularly where a rebate on tax is claimed. The scrutiny of VAT officials is notorious, and often charities and their trading companies will attract particular attention, perhaps because the regulations are very complex and unfamiliar to VAT officers, and what VAT officers do not understand they mistrust. Anything that involves a concession on VAT is likely to prompt a visit from the VAT inspector.

CHARITY MUST SATISFY

- THE CHARITY COMMISSION that it is acting in accordance with its trust deed
- THE INLAND REVENUE that its activities are wholly charitable, and not liable for tax
- THE CUSTOMS AND EXCISE that any VAT liability is met
- REGISTRAR OF COMPANIES if the charity is incorporated

The Charity Commission are most concerned to see the charity does what it is supposed to, in an appropriate manner, and that its resources are properly used. What a charity is set up to do is set out in its Trust deed. That is agreed with the Charity Commission before the charity can be registered. The Trust deed will also set out the powers of the charity, how it can operate, and this will generally include a declaration that the charity may not trade. The

CONDITIONS ON WHICH TAX CONCESSIONS ARE GRANTED TO CHARITY SHOPS

- profits must be applied for charitable purpose
- shops must be selling mainly donated goods
- shops must be run by charity not its trading company (for rate relief)

Note, if the shop is run as part of the charity's primary purpose then tax concessions also apply.

SALE OF DONATED GOODS BY CHARITY ARE NOT DEFINED AS TRADING

"Sales of donated goods at auctions, jumble sales and other venues are not regarded as trading. No liability to tax will therefore arise on the proceeds of these sales."

INLAND REVENUE.
Fund raising for charity (1994)

general rule is that if a charity undertakes any trading activity which is not part of its primary activity, as defined in its Trust deed, and which is permanent and substantial, then it should do so through a trading company. This is often misunderstood.

It would seem to the man in the street that a charity shop was both permanent and substantial, and if a member of the public is asked if a charity shop is 'trading' they would not even hesitate before saying 'yes'. For if a shop which sells things to the general public is not trading, what is? Like much in law, things are not what they seem. A charity shop, which sells donated goods where the profit is used for charitable purpose is defined by the Charity Commission and the Inland Revenue not as trading, but as fund-raising by converting donated goods into a more liquid asset, namely cash.

It is important to note that the sale of donated goods by a charity is not defined as trading. It is therefore an activity which can be undertaken by any charity without incurring the displeasure of the Charity Commission (who preclude charities from trading, except in pursuit of their primary purpose). Nor will there be a liability to a tax on profits, which the Inland Revenue might impose on any charity raising funds through trading (again, except in pursuit of its primary purpose) since the Inland Revenue agrees with the Charity Commissioners, that a charity shop is merely a means of converting donated goods to cash, and donations to charity are not taxed. A charity does not therefore need, nor should it, to operate its charity shops through a trading subsidiary, though several do.

There has been a great deal of misunderstanding as to whether running a charity shop is trading or not, and bad advice from solicitors and accountants, who should know better, has led many charities into the needless expense of setting up separate limited companies through which they operate their charity shops. This is bad practice. Charity shops selling donated goods can be, and indeed generally should be, operated directly within the charity, not through a subsidiary trading company.

Of course, a charity is bound by its Trust deed, its founding document, and can only operate a charity shop if permitted to do so in its Trust deed. It would however be a very peculiar Trust deed that directly forbade a charity converting donated goods into cash. To repeat, the usual proscribing of trading in the Trust deeds does not apply to charity shops, since in charity law, shops selling donated goods are not trading.

WHEN IS A TRADING COMPANY NEEDED

A charity shop may sell both donated goods and new goods, which have been purchased for re-sale. To take advantage of the tax and rates concessions the shop has to sell 'mainly' donated goods. This is defined by the Inland Revenue as over half. The sale of donated goods should be operated through the charity. If the shop sells bought-in goods, except on a very small scale and very occasionally, this activity must be run through a trading subsidiary.

The charity should, before it embarks on the sale of goods, consider carefully what the implications would be on its tax, VAT and legal position, and in particular whether it jeopardises its rate relief which is only available where mainly donated goods are sold.

For small scale trading activities where there would not be much profit on which to collect tax or which are very occasional, the Inland Revenue lays down, in Extra Statutory Concession C4, four conditions which, if met, mean there will be no liability to tax on profits on the trading activity. These conditions are:

1. The organisation or charity is not regularly carrying out these trading activities
2. The trading is not in competition with other traders
3. The activities are supported substantially because the public are aware that any profits will be devoted to charity
4. The profits are transferred to charities or otherwise applied for charitable purpose

In the preamble the Inland Revenue makes clear that it has in mind occasional one off events - it gives, as examples, "bazaars, jumble sales, gymkhanas, carnivals, and firework displays".

In the context of a charity shop, if the charity were on one occasion to buy stock for re-sale, and the quantity and value were both relatively small then it would probably be covered by the Extra Statutory Concession C4. It is when it begins to do so regularly that it becomes a trading activity, which has to be conducted through a subsidiary company.

PRIMARY PURPOSE TRADING

Some charities, for example, those running sheltered workshops, may want to sell products made by beneficiaries in their shops, possibly alongside donated goods. To do so would be part of the charity's work, its prime purpose, and it could be done by the charity itself, not through a trading subsidiary. There would be no tax on the profits, provided they were applied for charitable purpose. Rate concessions would apply.

The place of manufacture, or the fact that they are made by the disabled, does not make products 'charitable' and therefore able to be sold without tax or VAT, or by another charity as its primary purpose trading. To qualify for the exemptions, the products must be sold by the charity, made by its beneficiaries, and the profits applied for charitable purpose. Similarly, it cannot be argued that goods from Third World countries should be exempt, because they are made by poor people. For there to be any chance of falling within the category of primary purpose trading, the goods would have to be sold by a charity whose area of benefit was the Third World, and the products would have to be supplied by projects benefiting people who fell within the definition of beneficiaries. [Note the creation of employment is not in itself a charitable purpose, so there would have to be alleviation of poverty or distress.] Members of the public often assume that Third World goods are sold in charity shops as part of the charity's work, but generally these are handled by a trading company, with profits covenanted to the parent charity.

RATE RELIEF

Charity shops are entitled to rate relief in the same way as the premises occupied by charities for charitable purposes. The relevant legislation is the Local Government Finance Act, 1988, which replaced the Rating (Charity Shops) Act, 1976. The LGFA covers England and Wales. The rules are the same in Scotland, but Northern Ireland has a different system of charitable relief.

> ## CHARITY SHOPS QUALIFY FOR RATE RELIEF
>
> 80% mandatory
> 20% at the discretion of the local authority

Charities can claim rate relief of 80%, which means the charity only has to pay 20% of the rates. This relief is mandatory. The local authority has to give this concession, and then reclaims the cost from central government. Apart from the mandatory relief, the local authority may also give a further 20% discretionary relief, enabling the charity to pay no rates at all.

The LGFA section 64 (10) sets out clearly the conditions on which mandatory rate relief is granted.

> "A hereditament shall be treated as wholly or mainly used for charitable purposes at any time it is wholly or mainly used for the sale of goods donated to a charity and the proceeds of the goods (after any deduction of expenses) are applied for the purposes of a charity."

To qualify for the mandatory relief the rate payer must be the charity, or its trustees, not a subsidiary company. In fact, many charities which operate their shops through a subsidiary company do claim and are granted rate relief, but this is not technically correct, and has been challenged in the courts.

The shop must be selling mainly or wholly donated goods. The term 'mainly or wholly' is interpreted by the Inland Revenue as being more than half. The definition is very vague. It is presumably more than half by value, but it might be possible to argue that the measure should be physical quantity of stock. If the shop is selling goods made by the beneficiaries of the charity, or goods which are sold in pursuit of the charity's aims, for example, aids for the blind, then the project is run in pursuit of the charity's primary purpose.

A charity cannot simply accrue funds. If it does, without showing due cause, for example, that it is saving for some major project, then its right to rate relief and exemption from other taxation is likely to be challenged.

If a charity applies for mandatory rate relief and it is refused then it should take legal action against the local authority. Generally, the case is very clear cut. A legal challenge will concentrate the local authority's mind and the relief will be granted! Very occasionally an over zealous local government official will try to deny mandatory rate relief, for example, because the shop sells some new goods, which have been bought for re-sale. The charity simply has to show that these goods are less than half to qualify.

A reason for denying mandatory rate relief is that the rate payer was not in fact a charity. Registration under the 1960's Charities Act is proof of charitable status. If a charity is not registered then it would have to show that its purpose was charitable, and the organisation was capable of registration as a charity if it wished.

Claims for rate relief must be done in the rate year. The charity cannot be reimbursed if it has not claimed rate relief in the past. Once the local authority has given mandatory relief it will continue.

To get discretionary rate relief the charity has to apply to the local authority. Discretionary relief is not given automatically. A charity is more likely to get discretionary relief where it can demonstrate that it is benefiting the local inhabitants. The local hospice shop is almost certainly able to get discretionary rate relief whereas the large national charities may be less successful. As well as discretionary rate relief a charity can ask for the local authority for free refuse collection.

Rates are based on the rateable value of the premises multiplied by the uniform business rate. Any revaluation of the rateable value affects the amount payable, and it is sensible to challenge any increases which seem excessive. Although rate relief may reduce the burden, it makes it harder to sell or assign a lease if the rateable value is high.

Although charity shops are eligible for rate relief, there is no such help with water charges (previously called water rates). Even when there is no water to the premises the water board can charge water charges for sewerage and drains. Installing a water meter usually saves considerable funds. Ironically if the property has no water so cannot have a meter installed, there may be a liability to water charges calculated not on the consumption of water but on the rateable value of the premises.

WHY CHARITY SHOPS SHOULD BE RUN DIRECTLY BY THE CHARITY

Charities should operate their thrift shops (i.e. shops selling donated goods) within the charity, and not through a separate trading subsidiary.

Goods are donated to the charity for sale in the shops, and are assets of the charity not to be given away to a company. Of course, if a wholly owned trading subsidiary were the device by which the charity was making the conversion of the donated goods into cash, and its trustees satisfied themselves that the trading company was well run, and was getting the best deal for the charity when realising its assets, then there would probably be no objection to the use of a trading subsidiary. But the existence of a trading company does not relieve the trustees of their duty to ensure the charity's assets are used to best effect, it simply adds to their burden to see the charity *and* its subsidiary are both well run.

Since the relationship between the subsidiary trading company and the parent charity has to be at "arms length" (according to the Inland Revenue and the Charity Commission)

> ## CHARITY SHOPS SHOULD BE RUN BY THE CHARITY, NOT THROUGH A TRADING SUBSIDIARY
>
> - The goods are donated to the charity, and are an asset of the charity which it should not give away.
>
> - There is a substantial financial benefit, in the form of rate relief which is not available to a trading subsidiary.
>
> - The shops are using the charity's name, and it is prudent for the charity to control them as closely as possible.
>
> - Operating the thrift shops directly within the charity overcomes the problems of financing a subsidiary trading company.
>
> - Profits on the sale of the lease would be subject to capital gains tax if sold by the trading subsidiary. The charity would be exempt.

it may be prudent for the charity to charge its trading subsidiary a 'consideration' for the donated goods which are, after all given to the charity not the trading subsidiary. This had best be done toward the financial year end when the trading subsidiary has some notion of its profits, so that instead of paying over all profits to the charity, it pays over two payments one a consideration for the donated goods and the other payment for the profit. If the subsidiary company pays a consideration for the donated goods before it knows its results for the year, it may find it had paid over too much, and there were no profits (and a loss making trading subsidiary presents a real headache for a charity and its trustees). Also if the trading subsidiary errs on the side of caution and pays very little to the charity for the donated goods it may lead to complaints against the charity that it sold the charity's assets at too low a price. The net effect for the charity of the trading subsidiary making two payments to the charity, one for the donated goods, the second of the profits from the shops, is nil in financial terms. It is simply showing that the trustees and management of the charity are being very prudent in their stewardship of the charity's assets.

The Inland Revenue have argued that in the case of sponsorship a charity which gives benefit in return for a donation is in fact trading, and can be taxed, since it was not a 'pure donation'. It does not take a genius to work out that following its own arguments the Inland Revenue could challenge the payment from a trading subsidiary, which had been given the charity's donated goods to sell, as not being a pure donation. The larger the sum involved the more interested the Inland Revenue are likely to be. It is prudent to anticipate their objections.

The second reason charities, generally, should operate their thrift shops within the charity, and not through a trading subsidiary, is so that they can get rate relief. Section 64 (10) of the Local Government Finance Act, 1988 provides that premises used wholly or mainly for charitable purposes qualify for substantial savings on rates (properly called the Uniform Business Rate). There is mandatory relief of 80% of the business rate, and the remaining 20% can be waived, at the discretion of the local authority. Mandatory relief is available only to charities.

Note that the premises do not have to be exclusively selling donated goods. It is sufficient to sell mainly donated goods, and the Inland Revenue defines mainly as more than half. A shop could, for example, sell Christmas cards or wrapping paper which it bought in for re-sale, without jeopardising its entitlement to tax concession. The concession on rates is not allowed to trading subsidiaries, it is confined to charities.

In fact, there are many charity shops run through trading companies which have been getting rate relief, but the new procedures introduced with the Uniform Business Rate means that a charity has to fill in a form annually for any premises on which it is claiming relief, and has to state it is used wholly or mainly for charitable purpose by the charity. Are those signing the annual return prepared to perjure themselves for the sake of the 80% rate relief?

To run charity shops through a trading subsidiary, when it

precludes them qualifying for rate relief, could be argued to be negligent of the charity's trustees, since it involves a payment of funds that could come to the charity.

PROTECTING THE CHARITY'S GOOD NAME

An important purpose of running charity shops for any charity is that it puts its name on the high street, in front of potential donors. The public do not differentiate between the charity's activities and those of its subsidiary company. This makes it vital for charities to exercise control over the shops.

Generally members of the public do not have access to the information necessary to judge whether the charity achieves its objectives. Few can gauge the effectiveness of a medical research programme, or test the efficacy of one system of care for the disabled against the other. People are not so reticent about making judgements on whether they have been treated politely by those running the charity shop. They may feel the goods are over-priced or under-priced; that their generous gift of clothes has not been greeted with sufficient enthusiasm; that the shop is a filthy tip, and that by association, the charity's headquarters is likely to be a badly-run mess. It may be irrational but it is certainly true.

THE CHARITY COMMISSIONERS in their 1991 Report drew attention to the care a charity should exercise over use of its name.

"The Charity's name is a valuable asset. It is the means by which it is identified in the Central Register of Charities and to the public......... The name of the charity must not be exploited for non-charitable purposes."

That a charity shop generates publicity is a benefit, but it may also be a disadvantage, because of the image the individual shop may project. Is it prudent, in the circumstances, for the charity's trustees to allow shops, using the charity's name, and indeed in a position to jeopardise its good name, to be operated at arms length, through a subsidiary company?

It may be, in fact, that the control is as strict whether the shops are directly managed by the charity or by a trading subsidiary, but it may not be. Many of those responsible for running a chain of charity shops argue that wrestling control away from the charity is a prime reason for setting up a separate trading company. The

Those with queries on tax and charity should contact the Inland Revenue:

For England, Wales and Northern Ireland:
Claims (Trusts & Charities)
St. John's House
Merton Road
Merseyside L69 9BB
Telephone 0151 472 6044

For Scotland:
Claims (Scotland)
Trinity Park House
South Trinity Road
Edinburgh EH5 3SD
Telephone 0131 551 8294

interest of the charity should be paramount - it may be better served by keeping the enterprise under the presumably tighter control of a shops division within the charity as opposed to a trading subsidiary outside it.

If the shops, which use the charity's name, are run through a separate, though wholly owned company, it may be argued that the company is being given use of the charity's name, and should pay for that privilege. It may be prudent of the charity to levy such a charge - since the use of its name is certainly an asset, and the charity is not supposed to use its assets except for its charitable purposes. But whilst this may be a solution favoured by the Charity Commission, the charity should be aware that the Inland Revenue might argue that in charging for the use of its name the charity was trading, and its revenue, or the profit, from that transaction would be liable to tax, since it was not a donation. To avoid this any payments for the use of its name should be made to the charity as 'annual payment' (for the purposes of the Taxes Act) so that the charity can reclaim tax. To avoid this contemporary Morton's fork, it is perhaps better to operate the shops directly through the charity rather than through a trading subsidiary!

PROBLEMS OF INVESTING IN A SUBSIDIARY COMPANY

A charity may set up a subsidiary company through which to conduct any trading activity. The reasons for doing this are generally because the charity could not directly undertake the trading without incurring the wrath of the Charity Commission, nor escaping a liability to tax on the profits of the trade. To avoid paying tax on the profits of the trading company all profits are covenanted (or paid by Gift Aid or dividend) over to the parent charity before the end of the company's tax year, and as long as those profits are applied for charitable purpose the charity can reclaim the corporation tax. It is worth noting that to qualify for zero VAT rating on donated goods the company must transfer profits by covenant, not Gift Aid or dividend.

This device favoured by the Charity Commission and the Inland Revenue means that the charity loses no funds (to tax) and also the charity's assets are protected from the risks of trade, because the risk is taken by the trading subsidiary which is a limited company. However, the company has to be provided with working capital. Since this is not a charitable purpose there are clear restrictions on the charity's ability to invest in such an enterprise.

Charities have to spend their funds on charitable purposes to qualify for tax exemption. If they make investments these have to be qualifying loans or investments as defined in the Income and Corporation Taxes Act (1988)

PROBLEMS OF INVESTING IN A TRADING SUBSIDIARY

- funding the initial capital

- financing growth

- if loss is made

- gauging investment in commercial terms

Schedule 20. Loans to trading companies are not listed as such, so a charity has to get specific approval from the Inland Revenue for such loans to be recognised as qualifying investments. In practice it is easier to get approval from the Charity Commission and pass it to the Inland Revenue. To get approval the trustees have to show it is a worthwhile investment. Section 6 of the Trustees Investments Act 1961 makes it clear that trustees of a charity have to be more prudent in protecting the charity's assets than they may be when investing funds of their own. Lord Watson (Learoyd v Whitney 1883) commented:

> "Businessmen of ordinary prudence may, and frequently do, select investments which are more or less of a speculative nature: but it is the duty of a trustee to confine himself to the class of investment which are permitted by the Trust and likewise to avoid all investments of that class which are attendant with hazard."

Trustees, when considering investing in a subsidiary trading company, to provide it with working capital, have to consider carefully whether it is a good investment in terms of its expected return. Not only do they have to consider it, they should provide what is called a "paper trail", written evidence of their deliberations, and the calculations on which those deliberations and subsequent decisions were based.

The Charity Commission prefers a charity to fund its trading subsidiary through commercial borrowing, but it is generally unrealistic to believe the subsidiary company could get such a loan without the charity guaranteeing it, and the Charity Commission certainly would not normally sanction the guaranteeing of such a loan. Any charges on assets have to follow Charity Commission Guidelines. The trustees have to review the renewal of the loan at the end of the year, and any need to increase it to provide more working capital as necessary.

If the charity runs the charity shops directly within the charity, rather than through a trading company, the problem of providing working capital does not arise (except that the charity has to have enough resources to fund its shop operation).

If a trading company makes unplanned for losses (other than those it expected because of, for example, development or setting up costs) it creates enormous problems for the charity (and its trustees) because charitable funds must not be used to subsidise the losses of a trading company even though it is owned by the charity, uses its name, is perceived by the public as part of the charity, and gives all profits (when there are any) to the charity.

The economic recession of the 1990's has made trading more difficult, and the losses in trading companies more frequent. Whilst charities would not want to run charity shops at a loss, it may be that there is a temporary set back and the shops would become profitable very quickly once more. If the charity shops are run through a trading company and it makes a loss the charity would find it difficult to meet the losses so the company could continue. Operating the shops directly within the charity gives more flexibility.

CAPITAL GAINS TAX CONCESSION FOR CHARITIES

When property prices were rising, and there was a considerable demand for shop premises, charities which had bought the freehold or taken on the leases of shop premises found that if they were to close the shop they not only had no trouble re-assigning the lease or selling the property but they could also make a profit on the deal. If the lease was held by a trading subsidiary, there would be a liability to capital gains tax on the profit. If the charity sold the freehold or remaining lease at a profit it would be tax free, because charities are exempt from capital gains tax.

ARE SHOPS RUN BY A TRADING SUBSIDIARY BETTER MANAGED

It is thought that by having a separate company which has to have separate accounts, whose accounting method is determined by the requirements of the Companies Act, means that there is no chance of fudging the figures. It can be seen if the operation is profitable, or if it is being subsidised by charitable funds, which would be an improper use of those funds. If the shops are run directly by the charity, and they run at a loss, the charity should treat the expense as with any fund-raising costs - fund-raising is supposed to raise money, not lose it, and the trustees should put a halt to efforts which are consistently unsuccessful - unless they can show, and for their own protection minute, good reasons for continuing as part of a considered overall strategy.

There is always a temptation to cover up failure, and running the shops through a separate company makes it harder to cover up, because of the annual audit, which to comply with company law, has to be done by an independent auditor.

Generally a trading subsidiary of a charity pays over its profits to the charity each year, so retains no working capital, so each year it has to seek a loan from the charity, and this has to be considered by the trustees, to see if it is a sensible investment. Having a separate trading company concentrates the mind wonderfully, and means the operation's finances are probably more carefully scrutinised than if it were simply a division of the charity. This is a potent argument for a separate trading company.

Since a charity can operate shops selling donated goods without setting up a trading subsidiary it is prudent to run the shops within the charity. There are persuasive financial reasons for so doing

- rate relief
- exemption from capital gains tax on the disposal of leases
- sound management reasons - keeping closer control of activity
- public relations reasons - keeping closer control of the use of the charity's name
- it also gives better protection of the charity's assets, whether they are donated goods or its working capital

If the arguments for running charity shops directly within the charity are so strong why do some perfectly respectable, well-run charities choose to run their shops through a separate company. There are three main reasons - financial accountability, management independence and limiting liability of the trustees.

There is no reason why a charity should not organise its shops division so that its accounts are kept separately, and the same rigorous scrutiny of finances and performance built in. It is not necessary to have separate accounts, it just means overcoming the natural reluctance of those involved to make themselves fully accountable.

Running charity shops requires a particular type of skill. It is often felt by those given responsibility for running the shops that they are hampered by interference of others in the charity who do not really understand how the shops should be run but have a lot of options (often based on prejudice rather than any facts) and may use their senior positions to interfere.

By putting the shops into a company, with a manager in charge, it is quite clear where responsibility lies, and it becomes easier to avoid interference on a day to day basis. (The company's board meetings on which the charity's management will be represented may throw up a great deal of uninformed comment but at least the meetings are occasional).

It is really a question of good management, and this applies to all aspects of a charity's work. There seems to be a particular problem associated with any aspect of charity trading, 'the Christmas card syndrome'. Everyone feels they could choose the charity's Christmas cards, regardless of previous experience or any analysis of past performance or customer profile. Similarly, everyone seems to feel they could price donated goods, and will voice their complaints and views repeatedly, and attributing any lack-lustre performance of the charity shops to the failure to price the goods (or display them or appeal for them etc) as well they could. No wonder those in charge of charity shops want to be physically separated from the charity head office! In fact, all it means is they do not hear the carping, not that it is not going on.

> Managers of charities have got to learn that just as they do not allow uninformed criticism of, for example, the finance department, or the grants section to go unchallenged so they must not allow ill-tempered attacks on the running of the shops. The same standards of objectivity must be applied.

It is easier to understand and criticise shops than the work of the charity (there will always be something nasty to say about even the best run shop). The ethos in many, if not most, charities is to operate a hierarchy of moral virtue with the grant giving or care provision at the top, the service and management sections in the middle, the fund-raising below and the trading very much at the bottom. It is interesting that at Oxfam, where the income from charity shops is such a significant proportion of its income contributing more than £38 million to the charity in 1991, the charity shops are kept within the charity, not run as a separate company.

HOW TO TRANSFER SHOPS FROM A TRADING COMPANY TO THE CHARITY

If you are operating your charity shops selling donated goods through a company and want to bring the operation into the charity, how do you do it? The first question is to decide whether you want to keep the company or close it down completely. You may want to use the company (after all, it exists; you have paid to set it up and its relationship with the parent charity has been worked out). You may decide to run charity galas through the company, or the sale of bought in goods, or a Christmas card catalogue or corporate sponsorship. Think hard before you close the company down. You can keep the company dormant, as a shell for future use.

If you decide to close the company down (or wind it up, as the jargon has it) you need to sell off the assets, settle its debts and ask for removal from the Register of Companies. Winding up a company is very technical, and there is legal requirement to use a licensed insolvency practitioner, so you are forced to use professional advisers.

If you simply want to pull the charity shops operation out from the company and run it directly through the charity you have to transfer all the agreements that have been made in the company's name into the charity's name. When you realise that this includes the Electricity Board, the telephone company, perhaps the window cleaner, all employment contracts, the lease or licence to occupy, it is clear it is a very daunting task. You have to get the agreement to the change of everyone who has signed a contract with the company. Often the lessor of the shop may be very cautious in agreeing to any change in case it affects him adversely and you may have to pay his legal costs when he asks that his lawyers scrutinise the agreement.

LIMITING TRUSTEES' LIABILITY

The trustees of a charity are responsible for the running of the charity, and the protection of its assets. They are in a position of trust, and have a duty to exercise the same if not greater prudence in managing the charity's business than in handling their own. A charity's legal position does not afford the protection of limited liability, as does a company's.

As charity shop operations have got larger, there has been a nervousness about the extent of the charity's commitment of resources, and liability. For many charities this has led them to set up trading companies through which to operate their shops.

As charities moved away from simply occupying empty shops rent free under licence, on a temporary basis, and started to take on leases or even buy freeholds, the charities were seen to be putting charitable funds at risk. After all, they were taking on long term commitments, with some measure of risk. It was thought judicious by those solicitors and accountants advising charities, to recommend that the charity protect its assets by operating the charity shops through a limited company.

Throughout the 1980's this was even the advice given by some, though not all, of those at the Charity Commission. It is a very seductive argument. The weakness of it from the point of charity law is that it means giving away assets of the charity (donated goods). It involves financial loss to the charity (through loss of rate relief on the uniform business rate). It means a possible liability to tax on capital gains. It also means the use of the charity's name passes somewhat out of its control. Currently, the favoured method of running charity shops, or any primary purpose trading, is to keep it within the charity.

As their operations increase, in size and commitment, many charities have actually formed themselves as limited liability companies, limited by guarantee, to protect the trustees, who might otherwise find themselves financially liable. Liability of the trustees to ensure the prudent running of the charity and its financial affairs are not lessened by the establishment of a limited company, but it does give some protection of their personal assets if the charity incurs substantial losses not caused by their negligence.

There are particular problems with leases. The trustees sign the leases on behalf of the charity. They become personally liable for the rent and any service charges and repairs or dilapidation due under the lease if the charity defaults. If the lease is assigned by the charity and the subsequent tenant defaults then the obligations under the lease may fall back on to the charity. If the charity has gone out of business, but the lease still exists, the trustees could twenty years later find themselves being pursued for the rent. Some leases run for 99 years! Of course the best protection is not to take on long leases with substantial commitments.

It should perhaps be noted that under company law, the person running the company, for example the manager, may be held to be an 'effective director' or 'shadow director' and be liable just as the directors of the company are liable.

If a charity does not have limited liability itself, then when taking on leases, which are usually the main long term commitment, a clause should be inserted to limit the liability of the trustees, who are the signatories, to the assets of the charity. Other liabilities, for example, for product liability, should be dealt with by taking out an insurance policy. There are insurance policies designed to protect trustees, but these policies are largely untested and it is uncertain how much real protection they would afford.

VALUE ADDED TAX (VAT)

VAT (Value Added Tax) is a much misunderstood tax. Charities are not exempt from paying VAT nor from levying it on VAT-able transactions. Charitable donations are outside the scope of VAT, and that may be why the confusion arises and people believe charities do not pay VAT.

Like any company, a charity has to register for VAT when its turnover in VAT-able services or goods reaches the annual registration level fixed in each Budget. The level is sufficiently low to mean that most individual charity shops would have turnover in excess of the level at which they would have to register.

DONATED GOODS IN CHARITY SHOPS ARE ZERO VAT RATED

To qualify ...

- goods must have been donated

- sold by charity or its trading subsidiary

- profits have to be covenanted to charity (gift aid or dividended payments do not qualify)

Once registered the charity or company has to charge VAT at the stipulated level to its customers. Any registered body can claim 'inputs', ie the VAT it has been charged by its suppliers on supplies it needed to purchase to enable it to provide the service or goods on which it subsequently charges VAT. The 'input' tax is deducted from the 'output' tax (that is VAT charged to customers) and the balance sent, along with a declaration on turnover, input and outputs, to the Customs and Excise Office every quarter. Non-payment of VAT, like non-payment of PAYE, brings swift, punitive action. If a charity is registered for VAT it must deal with it promptly and accurately.

ZERO RATING IS THE BEST VAT POSITION BECAUSE CHARITIES

- can recover VAT paid
- do not have to charge VAT - keeps prices low

Note can claim input VAT on head quarter costs relating to the shops.

Donated goods sold in charity shops are zero rated. This is a very favourable tax position. The charity does not have to charge VAT on the goods to its customers, but because the goods are zero rated, not exempt, it may reclaim the 'input' tax it has been charged, on its quarterly VAT return. This concession extends to trading subsidiaries covenanting profits to the charity. (It actually extends to any 'taxable person' covenanting profits to charity). One strange anomaly to note is that the VAT concession extends only to taxable bodies which covenant the profits to charity, and is not available when profits are paid over by Gift Aid or by dividend. Charities should take care not to overlook this, as the otherwise useful device of paying profits by Gift Aid becomes much less attractive.

The zero rating on donated goods is worth a great deal to the charity, or its subsidiary, because it can reclaim the VAT it has been charged on costs relating to an individual shop, such as rent, surveyors' fees, telephone, window cleaning, cash till hire. It can also reclaim the VAT inputs on the central cost of operating the shop or shops.

THE ZERO RATING OF DONATED GOODS
is the most favourable VAT position. It may be an unwilling victim of the European community's harmonisation programme.

The charity should work out a formula on which to apportion central costs to each shop, for example, by number of staff employed in each shop, or size of the shop, or turnover. There is actually no one agreed formula, but the basis of apportionment should seem reasonable to the VAT-man. If in doubt ask for guidance from your VAT officer. The amounts of VAT that can be reclaimed are quite considerable - one charity reclaimed £750,000 on its head office costs, because it was able to claim retrospectively for several year's unclaimed 'input' tax.

A charity shop selling bought-in goods (ie. stock which it has purchased for re-sale) has to charge and account for VAT on those items. It must register if its VAT-able turnover reaches the level stipulated for registration. Both the sales of donated goods and the sales of bought in goods make up the VAT-able turnover, so it is almost certain the charity would have to register for VAT. Any donations, for example received in collection boxes in the shops, are outside the scope of VAT so should not be included. The zero rate concession extends to any manufacturer donating goods to the charity for sale in its shop. So, for example, if a manufacturer gives ends of lines, or a commercial shop keeper gives written off stock, they do not charge the charity VAT, but can claim input tax on the goods he donated (Items 1 and 2, Group 16 of the Zero Rate Schedule). Because the shop will be dealing with items which carry different VAT rates (donated goods zero rate VAT - bought in goods at full standard VAT rate) and these have to be recorded on the quarterly VAT return, it will be necessary to code the sales through the till, so at the end of each day the till will print out the sales of donated goods and those of standard VAT-able items. Note also that books and children's clothes both new and second hand are zero rated.

Those running the shop should remember that they will owe Customs & Excise the VAT charged on new goods, and set it aside. Though those nice men from Customs & Excise let you borrow their money, interest free, for several months, they are not indulgent towards non-payers, and do not offer extended credit facilities.

2
THE PREMISES

The Premises
- *where to open a shop*

Choosing a shop
- *location*
- *access*
- *size*
- *frontage*

Types of Tenure
- *rent free premises - licence agreements*
- *leaseholds*
- *freeholds*

Shop Layout and Design
- *outside & shop window*
- *display checklist*
- *inside of the shop*
- *layout*
- *shop fittings*

The Stock Room

THE PREMISES

WHERE TO OPEN A SHOP

For a charity considering setting up a charity shop or a chain of charity shops one of the first questions is 'where?' The locally based charity with a good knowledge of the area is in a much better position to make an informed decision than the national charity with a plan for 50 shop openings a year! The most sensible strategy is to open a shop in an area where there are strong, active supporters' groups. If the charity has no supporters' groups it may be able to identify any areas of concentration of donors through using its donor data base (mailing list of donors) who can be written to and asked if they would be prepared to help in the shop. The supporters' group should be consulted over the opening of the shop, because their involvement and support could be important.

The group may be sympathetic to the opening of a charity shop in its area, but might, because of the age or life-styles of its members, not in fact want to be involved in it. This gives the charity an opportunity to widen its appeal to different types of supporters in the area, who would like to work in a charity shop or help organise collections of donated goods, or take part in publicity drives for the shop.

If a supporters' group is absolutely against the opening of a shop in its area, then the charity has to gauge whether it wants to go ahead regardless. There may be good reasons for alienating the supporters group and introducing schism and internecine warfare into the charity's fund-raising efforts in the area, for example, where the charity's development is severely limited because the existing supporters' group is clique-ish, excludes and alienates new supporters, promulgates ideas inconsistent with the charity's declared aims, and generally is an embarrassment to the parent body. Opening a shop on 'their' territory may provide just the catalyst needed to promote their speedy departure in a cloud of umbrage.

If a good supporters' group is against the opening of a shop in their area it may be for good reason. For example, a major part of their fundraising efforts may have gone into jumble sales or car boot sales and they might fear that a shop would undermine these

---

THE KEY FACTORS IN CHOOSING A SITE FOR A CHARITY SHOP ARE

- location
- access
- size
- frontage
- rent
- facilities
- competition
- local supporters

efforts. They may feel a charity shop inconsistent with the image of the charity (and they may be right - museums, for example, should be very chary of selling old things, in case people think they are selling off part of their collection, or vouching for the quality of the items in some way). Groups may have a proprietorial attitude to their area, and not want the head office encroaching. Few supporters' groups actually see the head offices of the charity as providing them with services and support they need or want (however vital the charity's top echelons like to believe themselves).

The relationships between head office and supporters is difficult to manage. Headquarters' decision to set up a shop in the group's area may be seen as one more irritation, an example of "They set up a shop. We knew better, but they wouldn't listen, and now they are sorry, or they should be". So be careful, proceed with tact, develop listening skills, use the patience of Job, and the setting up of a shop should be a cause for pleasure for the charity's supporters in the area, because it will give them a focus for activity and increase visibility of the charity's name, which should make their fundraising efforts easier.

LOCATION

As the number of charity shops rises, the location of a shop has become more important in determining its success because it will be one of many. It is not as crucial as the manageress (or manager) but it makes their task very much easier. Generally, customers, and for a charity shop that means those donating goods as well as those buying them, owe no allegiance to any particular charity. They will go to whichever shop is most convenient. This is particularly true of those bringing in goods for sale, whereas those buying at the shop will become regular customers if the shop has a good range of stock and a pleasant ambience.

In the jargon of retailing, the best site for a charity shop is a secondary area. What does that mean? A prime shopping area is the busiest shopping area in a large town. To find out which is the prime shopping area or the secondary areas you can ask the local estate agents (if they are trying to sell you a shop lease they may exaggerate the desirability of a particular venue, so ask several agents). Typically a prime shopping site is one that shoppers will visit for a range of shopping, where they will in fact visit several shops, and combine shopping for pre-planned purchases with browsing and making impulse buys. Key retail planners in the USA claim that as most goods can be purchased anywhere, since the demise of the specialist shop, the key factor in retail success is attracting shoppers to a particular location - it is where they choose to shop rather than what they are shopping for that is important.

You may be able to identify the prime shopping area very simply by looking for key retailers, such as Marks and Spencer or a large branch of Boots the Chemist. If you want more specialist advice, the local authority will often have commissioned detailed surveys of retailing patterns in its area, including 'footfalls'. This will show the busiest thoroughfares and the routes most generally used by pedestrians. The Planning Department should have, or know of such surveys of the area.

> In prime shopping areas pedestrian flow is about 3,000 per hour.
>
> For a charity shop a pedestrian flow should be at least 300 per hour.

To find out which are the busiest areas, it is quite simple to organise a 'footfall count', to determine the pedestrian flow (number of passers by). For ten minute periods (one at what you think the busiest shopping time, say Saturday afternoon; one at the quietest time, say Monday mid morning and one at the average time, say Wednesday afternoon) multiplying by six will give you an hourly pedestrian flow figure - and adding the three figures and dividing by three will give an overall average. This is a very crude tool, as it does not take into account seasonal changes, weather conditions or external factors, but it does give some indication, and statistics always seem reassuringly authoritative. In prime shopping areas pedestrian flow is about 3,000 an hour, and it has been suggested that the minimum number of passers by for a viable charity shop is 300 per hour.

As well as considering how many pass the shop it is sensible to look at who they are. Are they businessmen walking briskly between office and station (not very likely charity shop customers) or are they mothers out shopping or students or old age pensioners. Number of pedestrians is one factor, the sort of pedestrians is also important.

A secondary site in a prime area is, say, just off the main high street, say two or three doors down in a side street, or at the ends of the prime shopping street. You do not want to be too far away from where the action is (the prime shopping area) to get the benefit of the large number of passers by. Ideally, the shop will be positioned to tempt in browsers and passers by, who will incorporate a visit to your shop with their other shopping. A nearby bus stop may also stimulate trade.

CHOOSE A SHOP IN A PRIME POSITION IN A SECONDARY AREA

OR

A SECONDARY POSITION IN A PRIME AREA

It may be advantageous to have a shop in the prime position in a secondary shopping area. That is an area where people may go to do day to day shopping, perhaps in a small town rather than a city. A drive through any small town in the country shows that large numbers of charities have chosen to site their shops in prime sites in secondary areas.

Choosing a good site is a talent. Those experienced and successful at siting their charity shops frequently refer to being guided by 'gut' feeling. In fact, they are simply using their experience to compare similar sites and discern the patterns of shopping in an area. Knowing an area helps. If you live there you probably can identify the busiest shopping centres. But beware relying on the advice of those who are not experienced retailers. To the casual observer an area might seem full of people, therefore full of potential customers. But those people may be rushing for a train, or working in the area, and do not use it for shopping. It is hard to convert people into customers in an area they do not consider for shopping. Generally shops do best when they are in shopping areas.

Since charity shops are selling low priced goods, and arguably this is a service to the poorer members of the community, would it not be sensible to site a shop in a poor area, where there are a large number of potential customers? In fact, generally charity shops in poor city centre sites do consistently badly. Some charities have as a matter of policy opened shops in inner city areas, through which to sell surplus stock from other shops - for example, Oxfam now has eleven Second Chance shops.

Location is not the main factor in determining the success of a charity shop. Generally, the management and in particular the individual manager is the most important factor. But location is important and a well run shop in a poor location can mean a great deal of wasted effort. If the same management and enthusiasm were transplanted elsewhere it would generate more trade and more profit. There is an old adage in the charity shop world which says the profitability of the shop correlates with the size of the Conservative vote at the General Election! There is a germ of truth in this, but a much higher correlation with good management.

ACCESS

Not all charity shops have to rely on pedestrian passers by. In some small towns it may still be possible to park on the main shopping street. This makes the existence of large numbers of charity shops in a small town (say with a population of 35,000) a more viable proposition than would at first appear - because the catchment area from which customers can be drawn is much widened, as people can drive to or near the shops, and stroll along, dipping in and out of the shops quite easily.

> **VEHICULAR ACCESS** is important not just for the customer but for the person bringing donated goods and the waste merchant collecting the unsold stock.

The ability to park even for a limited time outside a shop is an advantage, not just to the customer but even more so for those bringing donated goods. People will generally give to the shop to which they can most easily deliver and if they are not bringing in a single item, but rather several plastic bags or dustbin bags then convenience of parking, or collection, is a significant consideration.

Since a large quantity of the donated goods are going to be unsaleable, a major part of the charity shop operation consists of disposing of unsold stock. Much of this will be taken away by van to the waste merchant. Access is important. The waste merchant will not be inclined to pay good prices for sacks of jumble if he has to carry them far. It may even be hard to persuade him to take them at all. A policy of disposal of unsold stock has to be in place from the day the shop opens. It is essential to have vehicular access to the shop, not necessarily all the time, but so that collections of unsold stock can be made.

SIZE

The ideal size for a charity shop is probably 700 square feet plus a sorting area of 300 sq. feet. Some shops are bigger some are smaller. Charities can probably manage with anywhere between 350 sq. feet (plus a 150 sq. feet sorting area) to 1,500 sq. feet (plus 500 sq. feet sorting area). One large area can be divided subsequently, so a sorting area,

> **THE IDEAL SIZE** for a charity shop is probably 700 square feet plus a sorting area 300 square feet.

DREAM-ON CHARITY STORE

back door

store | kitchen | WC | WC

sorting area

door

shop window/street

lavatory and kitchen cubbyhole can be provided. Do not expect to walk in to premises and find everything just as you want it. Whilst you do not want to embark on major rebuilding works, particularly if you are simply occupying premises temporarily under license, you should expect, and include in your budget some refurbishment costs.

If a shop is very large you may be able to section part of it off, but remember you may find heating costs remain high. Also, you will probably be charged rates on the whole of the premises rather than the part of the premises actually in use, unless you manage to convince the local rating authority to charge rates only on the part of the premises in use. Even at 80% discount the local authority has to grant, this may be high. To strengthen your argument to the local authority, try pointing out that they can re-claim the 80% from central government - they cannot reclaim anything if the property is, in effect, unoccupied.

The overall size of the shop is one issue - its shape is another. Ideally, the shop will be rectangular with one short side taken up with the shop window and door. Running straight across the back will be a sectioned off area with the store room, kitchenette and lavatory. It is rare to find the ideal layout and, consideration should be given to how costly necessary adaptations will be.

Consider how comfortable and user friendly the shop feels. Much can be done with a coat of paint and proper lighting, but that can involve expense and it may be better to start with a well-lit, well ventilated, roomy, pleasant shop rather than constantly struggling to overcome its disadvantages.

FRONTAGE

The shop should have a prominent frontage on to the street of at least 15 feet on which the charity's name can be displayed, and the window used to display the shops wares. The frontage is the most effective way of letting customers know what is on offer in the shop. Not only do you advertise the name of your charity on the fascia board you also use the window to show the range and quality of goods you offer - what class of charity shop you are. Use the window to tempt people in.

Do not block off the view of your shop - potential customers are deterred by not knowing what happens behind the backdrop or pegboard of the window.

There are charity shops that have no shop window, that are upstairs or in basements, and they can succeed - but more resources have to be put into promotion and publicity, and this has to be budgeted for.

It is not impossible to attract customers in to a shop which does not have a street frontage, but it can be difficult, and a great deal of ingenuity may be needed. One can put out an 'A' board on the pavement (unless the local authority prohibits it). A projecting sign can be hung on a nearby building to direct potential clients (again local authority consent may be needed) a back lit sign or even a flashing neon sign could be used (but this will almost certainly need planning consent, and is certainly likely to arouse some opposition, if only from the local conservation group).

> ### THE SHOP FRONT SHOULD BE USED TO DISPLAY
>
> - the charity name
> - the shop's wares
> - show the inside of the shop

TYPES OF TENURE

There are generally three different types of tenure for a charity shop. The first is when a charity is lent the premises, free of rent or at a peppercorn rent, under licence, until the landlord lets or sells the shop. Secondly, the charity can agree to lease the shop for a specific period, at an agreed rent. Lastly, the charity can purchase the freehold (or long leasehold) on the premises. Which option is the best will depend on both the assets of the charity, the buoyancy of the property market and the opportunity. Often the best option for the charity would be a five year lease at a modest rent, with the option to renew, but property is not always available on those terms! In renting a shop one is constantly

> ### TYPES OF TENURE
>
> - charity lent premises, rent free, under licence, agrees to vacate on request
> - charity takes on a lease, and pays rent
> - charity buys the freehold

reminded that it is an imperfect world.

RENT FREE PREMISES - LICENCE AGREEMENTS

A shop may be empty because the landlord cannot let it at a commercial rent, or because he is trying to sell the whole building with vacant possession, or because he wishes to re-develop the site, or get planning permission for change of use. These are all good reasons why the shop is kept empty.

An empty shop is a liability to any landlord because it is at risk of being squatted and vandalised. It makes good sense to offer the vacant premises on a temporary basis, with no security of tenure, to a charity whose presence provides protection against squatters.

Owners have to pay rates on empty premises, though at a lower rate (no rates for the first three months and then 50% of the normal charge.) The increase in valuations for the introduction of the Uniform Business Rate has raised rates to very high levels. Charities can, if using the premises for charitable purposes or for the sale of donated goods, ie as a charity shop, receive rate reductions of 80% - and the further 20% can be waived at the discretion of the local authority. Thus by allowing a charity to occupy otherwise empty premises a landlord can save considerable amounts of money on the rates.

LANDLORDS MAY GIVE RENT FREE PREMISES BECAUSE

- it protects the shop against squatters and vandals

- it saves money on the rates

- it gives an opportunity to help charity

- it keeps the premises maintained

Apart from the warm glow of righteousness, that comes from helping a charity, the landlord also has sound business reasons for letting a charity occupy an empty shop. But how does a charity persuade the landlord, or even just get an opportunity to let facts speak for themselves? This is the crux of the problem for a charity trying to get use of a shop.

The property will normally be in the hands of an estate agent, and they may be completely uninterested in putting the charity in touch with the owner. They may simply not be prepared to do anything that involves work for which they are not paid, or it may be that they feel the charity shop will adversely affect their chances of letting the premises or that it will involve cleaning up and trouble getting vacant possession.

The owners are generally more helpful than the estate agents, it is therefore often best to try to contact the owner directly. To find out who actually owns the building, or has a long lease on it, ask the estate agent. Another, friendly estate agent may know who the owner is, or at least be able to elicit the information for you. If estate agents prove unhelpful you can track the owner through the land registry, for a small fee. (Solicitors usually make the search through the land registry but individuals can do so themselves). When approaching the owner emphasise the benefits (ie rate relief and protection against squatters) and the worth of your charity's work ("it would be wonderful if you could help the local hospice, or our children's play scheme or our aid programme"). Do not be aggressive. Try to make him feel good about his generosity. Remember you can never thank people enough (though do not be repetitive and tiresome).

Be prepared to listen to the reasons for not letting you use the premises, and counter the arguments - for example, he says he is not insured: assure him you will pay the insurance cost; he says he is worried about your not releasing the premises on request: say you will sign a license agreement which binds you to leaving at 24 hours notice; he says what about the cleaning up: say you will pay for any necessary cleaning at the end.

> ## EVEN FREE PREMISES HAVE COSTS
>
> - water rates
> - 20% uniform business rates
>
> Do not automatically say yes, you could lose money

Keep in touch with the owner once he has agreed to let you use the premises - perhaps twice or three times a year. Send a simple note saying how the project is progressing, how pleased you are to have the opportunity to have the shop, and how the charity is spending the profits (try to give a mental picture, for example, "We provided plants for the garden of the hospice"; "The money will buy seeds and tools for twelve refugee families"; "We are able to continue our research into heart disease, at Prof. James' Unit".)

You could put up a small notice on the premises, thanking the landlord for his generosity. Take care that the signage is not too large - it could be construed as advertising, and that could give rise to a liability to tax on the 'income' the charity has received (ie the value of the foregone rent).

If you are lent the shop it is sensible to have a licence agreement with the owner. The main points to cover are:

- What area is to be occupied

- Who is to be responsible for the maintenance of the property (the charity should not unwittingly take on responsibility for the building's structural maintenance). The charity's liability should be limited to responsibility for any damage it causes.

- How long a notice to vacate should be (try to get a month's notice, but agree to vacate immediately if necessary).

- Are there service charges. Who will pay them?

- Who pays the gas, electricity and water rates? You may persuade the landlord to meet these costs. Water rates can be very high - ask the Water Board not to notice you are there!

- Who will pay the rates? The landlord may agree to pay the 20% rate bill.

- Who will insure the building, including public liability cover and the plate glass shop windows?

- The charity will have to undertake to maintain the property in a tidy condition, and not allow bags of unwanted clothes to be stashed in such a way as to become a fire hazard.

- There should be an indication as to what purpose the premises may be put, after all, the landlord does not want to give the premises to the charity to find it then lets it be used for an acid house party.

- Who is liable for redecorating the premises during and at the end of the lease?

This is a sample licence

GENEROUS PROPERTY CO. LTD
CHILDREN & CANCER CHARITY

LICENCE TO OCCUPY
re: 21 Oxford Road, London W1

Generous Property Co. Ltd
Group Conveyancing Department
Tunstall Street
London SW3

The licence is made the _____ day
of _____ 199__

BETWEEN:
1. GENEROUS PROPERTY CO. LTD
whose registered office is situated at
Danesway, London SW3
(hereinafter called "the licensor") of
the one part
        and
2. CHILDREN & CANCER CHARITY
of 9 Bark Lane, London NW1
(herein called "the licensee") of the
other part

WHEREAS:
The Licensor is the owner of the
property described in the Schedule
hereto (and such property
hereinafter referred to as "the
Property") and the Licensee wishes
to occupy the Property for a limited
period

NOW IT IS HEREBY AGREED as
follows:

1. In consideration of the
obligations on the part of the
Licensee hereinafter set out the
Licensor hereby permits the
Licensee to occupy the Property
from the   day of   until the
(subject always to the right of the
licensor to terminate earlier as
hereinafter provided) whereupon
this License shall absolutely
determine

2.The Licensee hereby agrees with
the Licensor:

(i) To pay a licence fee of £1 to the
Licensor (if demanded)

(ii) Not damage injure alter or
otherwise harm in any manner the
Property save that the Licensee shall
be permitted to carry out non-
structural fitting out works

(iii) To keep the Property in a tidy
state and condition and forthwith to
repair any damage caused by the
Licensee to the Property and any
fixtures and fittings and make
suitable arrangements for the
prompt collection of any refuge or
other waste matter

(iv) Not to use the Property for any
purpose other than for retail
purpose and to comply with the
provisions of all relevant statutes
bye-laws and planning permissions

(v) To pay rates and for all
electricity and water consumed at
the Property and for any telephone
charges and telephone rental
incurred or charged during the
period of the operation of this
License

(vi) At the termination of this
Licence to cease occupation of the
Property and promptly to vacate the
same removing therefrom all items
belonging to the Licensee and to
reinstate the premises and to leave
the same in a clean and tidy state
and condition as provided aforesaid
free from refuse

3.The Licensor and Licensee hereby
respectively acknowledge:

(i) That this Licence is personal to
the Licensee and it shall not in any
way purport deal with the same or
confer any right by virtue of the
existence of this License any third
party over in respect of the Property
or any part thereof

(ii) This Licence shall not create the
relationship of Landlord and Tenant

between the parties hereto and shall not therefore confer upon the Licensee the right to occupy the Property on any basis other than as Licensee in accordance with the terms of this Agreement

4. If the Licensee at any time during the currency of this Licence fails to comply in all respects with the terms and conditions hereof then without prejudice to any right of the Licensor which may have accrued prior thereto the Licensor shall have the right upon giving seven days notice in writing forthwith to terminate this Licence whereupon the Licensee shall immediately cease to occupy the Property and to remove therefrom all persons and items under its control leaving the Property clean and in a tidy state and condition as aforesaid

5.This Licence may be terminated by either of the Licensor or the Licensee giving to the other at least two weeks previous notice in writing to that effect and in the event of such notice being given the Licensee shall vacate the Property on or prior to the date specified in the notice and leave the same in the condition specified in clause 2(iv) of this Licence

6.The Licensee hereby agrees that if when the Licensee ceases to occupy the Property and having removed all items and persons under its control therefrom the Property and its fixtures and fittings therein are not in at least as good a state of repair and condition as same now are in (fair wear and tear and damage by insured risks excepted) then the Licensee shall forthwith pay to the Licensor the sum reasonably required to restore the Property and the fixtures and fittings to such condition and that in event of any disparity the sum shall be determined by an independent Chartered Surveyor appointed by the Licensor whose decision shall

be binding upon the parties hereto

7.THE LICENSEE HEREBY AGREES to indemnify the Licensor in respect of any cost claim charge expense or otherwise incurred by the Licensor in respect of or resulting from the Licensee carrying on its business at the Property and the Licensee further agrees with the Licensor to maintain insurance cover in respect of any liability which might arise to a third party as a result of accident injury loss or destruction or any other damage occurring as a result of the Licensee carrying on its business at the Property and will produce to the Licensor on demand a copy of such insurance policy and a receipt for the last premium due thereunder

8.(i) The Licensor is entering into the Agreement only upon the express agreement of the Licensee that all warranties conditions guarantees or representations express implied statutory or otherwise relating to the Property which is the subject matter of this Agreement are hereby excluded and the Licensor shall not be liable for any loss damage expense or injury of any kind whatsoever consequential or otherwise arising out of or due to or caused by any defect or deficiencies of any sort in the Property

(ii) The Licensor does not warrant that the Property can be used for the purpose for which the Licensee will (or intends to) use the Property

As WITNESS the hands of the parties hereto
THE SCHEDULE
ALL THOSE premises know as 21 Oxford Rd, London W1
SIGNED by

on behalf of the Licensee
in the presence of:

Even though the premises are offered free of charge the water charges and 20% of the uniform business rate can add up to very substantial amounts. Ask what these are before you agree to take on premises. It could be as much as £20,000 p.a. Do not be browbeaten into accepting free premises - there are still costs attached and it is better to say 'no thank you' rather than saying 'yes' because you do not wish to give offence, and find you are losing your charity's money. A tactful 'It is so kind of you, but the uniform business rates and water rates between them probably mean we would not be able to make a profit' is the best way to refuse without giving offence, or the impression that the charity does not need money or cannot be bothered working for it.

RENTING PREMISES - LEASEHOLDS

Shop premises may be available to rent for a fixed period, at an agreed rent. Leases can be for very short periods, say for 6 months or for very long periods, say for 99 years! Generally a lease will have provision for rent reviews every three or five years usually on an upwards only basis so there is no provision for the rent going down.

If you sign a lease you are agreeing to pay the rent and service charges and other costs for the whole of the specified period. This is usually a substantial commitment, and should not be lightly undertaken. It is possible to assign a lease, but this will depend on the buoyancy of the market.

Throughout the 1980s charities often made profits from selling their shop leases, but during the recession of the 1990's, found that not only could they not sell the shop leases at a premium, but they could not find anyone willing to take on the shop lease when they wanted to give up the premises.

If you are signing a new lease whilst it would normally allow you to dispose of it through assignment, it is important to know that through an anomaly of English law, the person or body signing the lease remains liable to the landlord for the rent if the

> ### WHEN SIGNING A LEASE OR BUYING A FREEHOLD TO SAFEGUARD YOUR TRUSTEES
>
> • have a solicitor check the lease
>
> • have the property surveyed.

person to whom the lease is assigned fails to pay the rent. So, for example, you sign a new lease on a shop, but sell the lease to another company because you decide to re-locate to a better position. That company goes bankrupt, and the landlord then

---

MAINTAINING THE PROPERTY

- do a regular property check
- look at the requirements of the lease
- make clear who has authority to deal with repairs
- have a report and authorisation procedure

demands the rent from you as the head leaseholder. Try to negotiate a clause excluding this in the original lease. It is prudent, and increasingly usual, for those reassigning a lease to ask for a guarantor, so if the business fails the liability does not revert to them.

There are two safeguards against being tied into a shop lease. One is to have a very short lease - say for three years, and the other is to insert a break clause - which would allow you to terminate the lease on a period of notice. Your ability to insist on either or both of these conditions, depends on the state of the property market. In times of recession the landlord will be prepared to make deals he would not have to consider when demand is high.

Do not be panicked into signing a lease that does not suit your needs, or commits you to high levels of spending, because the market is buoyant and shops seem to be snapped up, and higher offers made. Many charities have lost money on their charity shops because they have rushed into taking expensive leases to meet expansion targets. Shops should be taken when the property market is not at its peak. If there is a boom, and rents soar, you can be sure it will be followed by a slump.

Always calculate what rent you can afford on the basis of what sales you expect to make. For shops selling new goods the usual target for rent is 10-15% of turnover. It is sensible to budget for all occupancy costs totalling around one quarter the income of the shops. Occupancy costs include any rent, rates, insurance, heating, lighting, water rates and building maintenance. For many charities the occupancy costs are nearer to 30%.

The advisability of taking a shop lease should be considered not just in the context of what other shops cost (though, of course, you have to know whether you can compete at all with other shopkeepers) but whether the rent is realistic for your purposes. Charity shops have much lower costs, since in conventional retailing half the turnover goes in paying for stock. They may also have lower staff costs, because they can mobilise volunteer labour, and they also make savings on rates and VAT. But their budget is much lower than other retailers. Remember that rent is only one part of your occupancy costs. The lease will almost certainly contain other charges made by the landlord, either service charges or a share of the building's maintenance or insurance cost. These can be startlingly high, and add as much as 50% more to the rent. Also, although there is relief on rates (80% mandatory and 20% at the council's discretion) there is no relief on water rates, and these are often very high. (Investigate the possibility of installing a water meter, it is often cheaper.) Insurance rates are soaring, and in some areas your landlord will require you to take out insurance against terrorist attacks. All these costs eat into profits.

Most leases stipulate that the tenant has to keep the property in good repair. In some cases the tenant simply undertakes to leave the property in the same condition as they found it, in others there will be a full repairing lease, which means the tenant has to pay for all maintenance and renewals, even when these are caused by the landlord's previous neglect - for example, dry rot caused by a previously neglected leak. Make sure you know what liability you are taking on.

Make sure the landlord gets any previous tenant to pay for any dilapidations (that is repairs for which they were liable under their lease). This quite usually will mean the shop can be fully decorated. Often the landlord will agree to your getting the decorating done as part of your refurbishment but give an allowance towards it (he can afford to be generous since he gets it back from the previous tenant). It makes sense to have any property surveyed, and to use the survey as a negotiating tool.

If you are signing a lease it is sensible to use a solicitor to check it. The trustees of the charity will normally be the signatories, on the lease. Under the Charities Act trustees can be held personally liable for the proper management of the charity and its assets, so it is only fair to take proper legal advice before the trustees commit themselves and the charity. The lawyer should be asked to ensure that the lease states that the trustees liability is limited to the assets of the charity. This is particularly important when a new lease is being signed because of the continuing liability for any subsequent assignee defaulting.

> **WHEN DRAWING UP A LEASE** ensure trustees liability is limited to the assets of the charity.

Should the lease be taken by the charity or its subsidiary trading company? The advantages of the charity holding the lease are firstly, that in the event of the lease being sold the charity, but not its trading subsidiary, is exempt from capital gains tax and secondly, rate relief is available to a charity not to its trading subsidiary.

In theory the trading subsidiary could take the lease and sub-let to the charity or grant a licence to occupy (not assign the lease). Of course, the lease would have to allow for sub-letting or granting of a license. This device would protect the charity's assets, as the commitments under the lease would fall to the company not the charity. The main disadvantage is that the landlord may be reluctant to let to a company with no assets or reserves (a trading subsidiary has to pay over profits before the year end to avoid tax so cannot accumulate assets) and may ask for the parent charity to act as a guarantor. Acting as a guarantor is a very unattractive option for a charity, as it commits charitable funds to the under writing of a trading company, and it could be argued that this is a breach of trust. A charity may not subsidise its trading subsidiary, even when the subsidiary is operating charity shops, which could be run through the charity.

The device of the company taking the lease and sub-letting to the charity may seem more attractive in theory than in practise. Landlords are likely to be chary of agreeing to arrangements designed to make it easier for the tenant to stop paying rent in the event of poor trading.

BUYING PREMISES

It is only worth buying premises if the charity is certain that the property is offered at an advantageous price; that the shop is in the right location for its long term success and of course that the charity can spare the funds for this long-term investment.

It is not the job of a charity's trustees to speculate on the property market with the charity's resources. Charities are set up for specific purposes set out in their trust deeds. The whole *raison d'être* of a charity is that money can help the problem, for example through grant-giving, or research, or the provision of services. A charity's exemption from tax is granted because of the good works done for the good of the community. If the charity does not spend its funds for charitable purposes, but rather accumulates funds and invests them, and thereby continues to accumulate them, the Inland Revenue will quite rightly levy taxes, on the grounds that the funds exempt from tax are not being used for charitable purpose.

Charities can act prudently and accumulate reserves to ensure that their work can continue. Indeed if the charity provides continuing care, for example, in old people's homes or day centres then it has a duty to set aside some funds to enable it to meet its commitments. These reserve funds may, in small part, be used to purchase shop premises, from which the charity could sell donated goods. Even if the money is available to purchase the premises the trustees must satisfy themselves that the purchase is a good investment; that the amount of interest foregone on the capital spent (which after all would otherwise be invested

BUYING PREMISES may give the opportunity to sell the premises subsequently at a profit - but charities have in the property slump found themselves unable to sell property except at a considerable loss. Property prices do not always rise.

perhaps in a building society or on the money markets) would be less than the amount of rent that the charity would have to pay to secure the premises - allowing, of course, for the value of the freehold. The trustees should not base the decision to purchase on the expectation that property values will rise. It is not inevitable and whilst more likely than gambling on the horses, it is still too risky a use for charitable funds.

The circumstance in which it is perhaps most sensible to purchase the freehold of a shop are when the charity has been a tenant for some years, is operating the shop at a good profit, and has the opportunity to buy rather than pay rent. Then the charity is in the best position to judge whether the purchase is a good idea, and how soon the investment will be repaid.

When purchasing use a solicitor to make all the usual searches. Any redevelopment schemes for the area, which would affect trade, should be revealed at this stage. Buying premises involves a long-term commitment to the shop (unless one is trying to speculate on a rise in the property market - and one should not) therefore consider the long-term development of the area. Are shopping patterns likely to change? Is there a traffic management scheme planned which will improve or reduce the number of people passing the shop? Is the character of the town changing? Is there a shift in population away from the area? Is unemployment likely to rise in the vicinity? If there is one major employer in the area what are the long prospects for that industry? Thinking about the likely developments may lead to second thoughts, or at least a measure of indecision.

Buying a shop can be a really serious mistake. You may not want to continue to run a shop, and be stuck with premises you can neither let nor sell. That means tying up the charity's assets.

The public are not always well-informed as to the advisability of buying shop premises. Years ago Oxfam bought the freehold of the shop in Hampstead which it had rented for years. It has turned out to be a very good investment, and the shop has expanded and trades profitably. But some residents expressed the view that if Oxfam is so hard up and always appealing for funds for starving people how come they can afford to buy a shop. Oxfam could argue justifiably that they were prudently saving rent and therefore husbanding resources, but it does take the immediacy out of the appeal!

SHOP LAYOUT AND DESIGN

THE OUTSIDE AND SHOP WINDOW

A charity shop should not look lavish, but nor should it be shabby. Even if the shop is to be occupied temporarily, try to get the outside up to a minimal standard of cleanliness and order. Get the window cleaned (professionally) and the paintwork washed down.

The name of the charity should be prominently displayed outside the shop - usually on the fascia board, but possibly on the window and in a hanging sign. You may need planning permission for a hanging sign (particularly in a conservation area) and 'A' boards are not allowed by some local authorities. They may give 30 days notice to remove the offending sign, but some local authorities use summary justice - and a notice to pay a fine (and it can be substantial) may be the first thing you know about your breaking the law, so check first!

Some charities devise what they presumably judge is an attractive name for their chain of charity shops - often a flower or bird name. This winsome approach seems foolish, and mawkishly sentimental. Why choose a name you have to explain and establish, when you could use the opportunity to reinforce awareness of your charity's name? There are of course, some cases in which a charity's name is cumbersome or dated, when abbreviation can help, and some charities, particularly sectarian ones, have adopted the trick of obscuring their true identity behind more neutral names. Generally a charity is will advised to take the opportunity of promoting awareness of its name and its cause by displaying it on the shop.

A fascia board is not a big space, and clarity should not be sacrificed to the wish to explain the cause. The name of the charity, perhaps with a smaller by line if the name by itself is not well enough known is probably all that is needed. The shop sign should be professionally painted (perhaps the sign writer may donate his labour, or at least offer to reduce his fee). To find a sign writer look in the Yellow Pages. Find a shop fascia you like and ask him to follow the same style.

CHECKLIST OF INFORMATION FOR THE SHOP FRONT

- name of the charity
- mission statement (if needed)
- shop opening hours
- telephone number
- words 'a registered charity' after the correct name of the charity (required by the Charities Act)

The large charity shop chains have all put a great deal of energy into having logos and house colours, designed by top design groups. Having a logo does not put more money in the till! It tends to make the staff of the charity feel better, and hopefully work better. But it is not a prerequisite of running a successful charity shop. Presentation is not just about having a logo. It is more about maintaining high standards of housekeeping. The shop design may look wonderful on the drawing board but once the local staff and volunteers have stuck their home made signs all over the window (crookedly) and decided to keep the lights switched off to save money the impact will be lost.

When you are working out the appearance of your shop front, design is perhaps too grand a word, allow for the signs you may wish to put up for particular occasions - for example a special appeal for certain types of donated goods. ("Unwanted Christmas presents gladly received" or "Collection point for the Bosnian appeal"). Make sure the signs will not obliterate the display - in fact, provide the shop with posters on which the message can be written. They can be inexpensively produced on a photo copier from quite simple computer generated design. You may even have a notice board in the window or on the door, so that the plethora of hand-written messages can be contained. It is no bad thing to have a display of 'postcard' messages (the classic "postcard in the newsagent's window") as it may draw people to the shop.

What information will you need to have outside your shop? Firstly, the charity's name prominently on the fascia board. If your name is not known than have a slogan (a mission statement) explaining what you do. On the door to the shop, or at one side of the window, have the shop opening hours. A requirement of the Charities Act is that the fact that solicitations are being made on behalf of the charity should be clear - so the words 'a registered charity' should be displayed after the charity's correct name. (This should be on the door or window rather than the fascia board). The telephone number should be displayed, so potential donors can call up to arrange deliveries. If you can arrange collection of donated goods advertise the fact on your window.

Whatever you decide to have in your window make sure it is clean, both inside and out. Negotiate a contract with a local window cleaner. Do not be tempted to use volunteers to clean windows if it involves standing on anything other than the ground! It is not a good idea to have people standing on chairs or ladders, with the risk of them falling off and injuring themselves. It is particularly irresponsible if they are elderly volunteers. If the shop is on a busy road, with traffic, there will be a great deal of dust and you will need to clean the paintwork at regular intervals, particularly ledges where the dust will gather.

The shop window is very important. It is your way of showing what type and standard of product you are offering. Your way of presenting the merchandise shows how you regard it and gives it value. If you pile things up in the window you are giving the message - we have lots of things, come and rummage. If you treat the stock very seriously - one featured item in a window, you are proclaiming that you consider the item as being worth featuring. Think about how other shops treat their window displays. This shows some of the options you have. Harrods, for example, will have relatively few items, displayed with substantial amounts of 'props', to tell a story or set a theme. Compare a department store's sale window with their more usual displays. More items will be displayed, 'props' will be dispensed with - the theme is that there is a lot to buy inside the store at reduced prices.

A high-class department store seals off its windows, other shops, for example Woolworths, virtually dispense with window displays. They use windows to show the interior of the shop. Generally people are nervous to enter the unknown, and if you block off the interior of the shop by sealing off the window display then you may deter customers. Either keep the window free of display so customers can see into the shop, and see what is on offer, or use part of the window for a display, but keep a view into the interior.

Try to provide a dummy or some form of display stand which can be easily used. Look at other shop windows for ideas on how to improve and vary your display. It is no good expecting your volunteers to have window dressing skills (though many feel they have the potential, and love to have a go!) try to make the system fool proof.

Remember to look at your shop window as a passer-by on foot and from a bus or car. Check on the appearance of your shop on a daily basis. See that nothing in the window has been disturbed and not put back correctly. Never refuse to take anything out of the window display for a customer, after all the whole point of the display is to sell the goods, not to have a window display, and be cheerful about it! Have a note of the size of any item on display, but do not be tactless and tell a customer "Oh it's a size 12 it'll never fit you". It is not for you to tell a potential customer she is fat. For all you know she is buying it for someone else!

The shop window is the first impression of the shop. It gives potential customers information on what is on sale, and its likely quality and cost. What you put in the window display, not just how you display it is an important part of that message. Above all the shop window must be welcoming, not forbidding. It should not be tired and dusty, with stock drooping on hangers. People should not be ashamed to admit they shop there, or hope not to be seen entering.

Buying second hand clothes can be a clever way of dressing with individuality or a way of dressing cheaply. Your shop window should

SOME OF THE KEY ELEMENTS OF SUCCESSFUL WINDOW DRESSING ARE

- Change the window weekly or fortnightly at least to maintain interest, and show your stock is constantly changing.

- Display in a triangle.

- Use a theme either colour in which case try to stick to two colours for example, black and white. Or seasonal theme - eg Halloween, Back to School, Easter Bonnets.

- Try to mix clothing and bric and brac, to show the range of goods on sale.

- You are not selling the price tickets - stock should be priced and labelled, but the item not the price ticket should be the first thing to catch the eye.

- Follow the Greek Golden Rule, it is more pleasing to the eye, and appears more balanced to see odd numbers of displays than even. For example, one or three or five figures is better than two or four.

- Fill the vertical window space, do not put everything on the floor so the customer has to look down. Build up the display to the customer's eye level. (5'6" from the pavement should be the top of the display).

- The eye travels horizontally not vertically and from left to right then downwards. Therefore the focal point of the display should be to the right of the window.

- The shop window is usually a large space and needs quite broad-scale treatment. Take care to avoid small puddles of stock.

emphasise the fun aspect of shopping in a charity shop, not the money saving. People buy things because they like them (and because they are a bargain). If they do not like the look of them they will not think them a bargain. The purpose of your shop window display is to enhance, not detract, from the merchandise, and you must ask yourself every day, does the item in the window look better or worse than it would when worn. If the answer is worse, change the window!

THE INSIDE OF THE SHOP

Shopping has become a leisure activity over the last decade. People will go out shopping not just for specific needs, but on the look out for items which take their fancy. Attracting the browser into the shop, and tempting them to buy something once they are there is the key to successful retailing. This is as true for the charity shop's customer as it is for a department store or gift shop.

Surprisingly few customers in charity shops are buying because they really need the item, for nearly all the purchase is an extra blouse or shirt or coat which gives them the variety at relatively low cost. This means no one has to come into your shop. They may be able to choose another charity shop, or buy at a car boot sale or simply go without. What will attract them into your shop in the first place is the outside appearance, but what will turn them into a regular customer is the quality of the stock, the friendliness of the staff and the ambience of the shop.

Loyalty to the charity cause is very low on the customer's list of reasons for shopping at a particular charity shop. Most charity shop customers are indifferent to the charity's cause - whilst they are pleased that the profit goes to charity they are not particularly discriminating as to which charity, and if interviewed in a charity shop will often be unable to name which charity the shop is run by (often the charity shop will be generically described as "the Oxfam").

The layout and design of the shop are obviously very important in

---

BUILD CUSTOMER LOYALTY

- by friendly service
- good, frequently changing stock
- good variety of stock
- pleasant atmosphere
- good, clean shop layout

creating the right atmosphere. The shop has to be "easy to shop". It has to be laid out in such a way as to make sense to the customer. The aisles, or spaces round fitments, have to be wide enough to allow the customer to circulate freely, and be passed without being jostled. If you do not create an atmosphere in which the customer feels physically comfortable they are not going to spend time in the shop - and in a charity shop with its variety of stock time has to be spent to search out the right items.

The walls should be painted a restful colour - usually a warm shade of white is best. In a dark shop without much natural light, white walls or ceiling can be attractive, but generally off white is more restful. Do not, except in exceptional circumstances which one cannot actually imagine, use strong colour on the walls. The stock, not the shop, should be what catches the eye. If you inherit a shop with brightly painted walls or wallpaper simply paint over in a neutral shade.

Shoppers feel more comfortable and will linger longer if the floor is not hard (say slate or linoleum). Consider the options of carpet, carpet tiles, cork or wood. Sometimes if you lift up a carpet there is a wood plank floor that can be sanded and sealed, and which is virtually maintenance free. If using carpet, choose heavy duty quality, and budget to replace it fairly frequently. Whatever the floor covering, it should be of a neutral colour preferably with a slight pattern which will not show the dirt or bits of lint.

Provide the staff with the means of keeping the floor clean - either a heavy duty industrial vacuum cleaner or a brush and pan for wood, cork or linoleum floors. Take care that the floor covering is not frayed, so that staff or customers could trip, and similarly make sure no electrical wires are trailing across the floor to act as a trip wire for the unwary.

The greatest fault in charity shop display is poor quality lighting. Fluorescent lighting is harsh, and creates a hard-edged atmosphere in which people do not generally want to linger. Lighting with conventional

LIGHTING in charity shops is usually too dim. Use halogen lighting for the most natural light.

bulbs is usually inadequate. Using spot lights whilst cheap to maintain is actually an expensive system to run, as the spotlights need to be changed frequently, and the fittings seem to burn out and need replacing every few years. Low voltage lighting is expensive to install, but economical on consumption of electricity. It gives the best quality of light. Replacement bulbs are expensive, though supposedly long lasting, but should be bought in bulk at about one third of their normal retail price.

The shop will need heating and hot water to the basins and sink. There are three rules on heating, firstly that it be safe, secondly that it is flexible so you can have heat when needed (this is important in our changeable climate) and thirdly that it is economical to run. Gas central heating, may be appropriate, if the radiators can be installed without encroaching on selling space. A hot air system, with an overhead curtain heater above the shop entrance may be a good choice. Ease and cost of installation is clearly going to be an important factor. In temporary premises heaters using calor gas may be an alternative, but make sure they are well away from customers, and have fixed safety guards around them, because there is a risk of scorching clothes that brush against them. As well as the shop area the back sorting area will certainly need to be heated. Because of the risk of clothes being dropped on to the heater electric bar fires or paraffin or gas stoves with a naked flame should not be used.

HEATING must be

Safe - in all circumstances

Flexible - giving heat when needed

Economical - to install and run

LAYOUT

The layout of the shop will dictate to the customer how they can 'walk' the shop. Most customers turn naturally to the right and move clockwise. By placing stands and siting island displays you are determining the route the customer will most naturally take. A strip of carpet of a different colour can also act as a subconscious pathway. If the shop is very deep, so the customer has the choice of going half way down the shop, and turning round without going to the bottom section, you can overcome this by blocking the way with central islands or using the trick of the supermarkets, by siting the most wanted stock at the back of the shop. With either device you run the risk of deterring the potential customer from bothering at all. Make sure your display at the back of the shop is really attractive, and well lit. Do not make the isles an obstacle course. Remember, the customer does not really need what you are selling, and can be deterred.

The cash desk should be near the door. This is a logical place, and should make it easier to prevent people walking out without paying. The cash desk should be positioned so that the whole of the shop can be seen by the person behind the till. It may be possible to build a raised dias about six inches high, to increase visibility - make sure it is wide enough so people behind the cash desk have enough space to move around without tumbling off!

Do not have a cash desk that the staff become imprisoned behind. You want staff to move out from behind the till to serve customers and tidy the shop, and need to overcome the natural tendency to cluster round the till. Some cash desks make this inevitable by making it difficult for the staff to come out from behind counter. The till does not have to be defended like some erstwhile holy grail - it can be immobilised by removing the key, so a thief could not open the drawer. If the till is so near the open door that you are afraid it might be snatched, screw it or weight it down.

Have enough space below the cash desk, or to one side of it, to keep packaging material close to hand. You do not need to have a bespoke cash desk - you can use a table, put the till on top, and keep most of the surface clear for packaging. Bags and equipment can be kept below the table in a filing cabinet or cupboard or small bookcase.

THE SHOP FITTINGS

The fittings you use and how you display the stock help create the atmosphere of the shop. If you want to attract a young, student crowd, who want cheap clothes, and a funky look, then do not use chrome shop fittings - but rather try to use old dummies and hat stands, draping feather boas or long scarves round the neck. Invest in a few peacock feathers to put in a jar. Perhaps use an Edwardian wardrobe to help create the right atmosphere. Hang clothes inside, and keep the door propped open. If you want to attract a more elderly, conservative clientele, make the shop look more orderly. Try to use conventional shop fittings. Calm the customers, make them feel that nothing unexpected is going to tumble down on them.

The growth of chains of charity shops has meant more and more shops are opened to a standard formula. They use a standard fascia; the walls are covered in white grooved board, into which chrome rails can be slotted. The fluorescent lighting is fitted under a concealed board above the rails, like a counter top in a fitted kitchen. The shop design and fittings try to contain the enthusiasm and act as a barrier to the initiative of the shop manageress and volunteers. As a result the shops become rather sterile. Much of the fun is taken out of the shopping, which is a shame, but it gives the national organiser a much greater sense of being in control and makes it easier to ensure shops maintain a prescribed standard of cleanliness, organisation and management.

If the bulk of your sales will be of donated clothing most of it will be half-length (for example blouses, skirts, trousers, jackets) so double-tier your fittings so you can get an upper and lower rail rather over providing for full-length garments and wasting space. Coat rails, used by garment manufacturers, though an inexpensive solution to providing hanging space have two disadvantages. Firstly, they are generally full-height, so only suitable for full-length clothing such as coats and dresses. Secondly the protruding feet, on castors, are likely to trip up customers and staff and lead to accidents.

> **DO NOT CRAM THE RAILS WITH STOCK.** Rails should be two thirds full. When stock is pushed along the rail - one third should be empty.
>
> Aim to display 2 items per sq. foot of display area.

Since all your stock is different, it is important to display as much of it as possible. This does not mean jamming into the rails so tightly that the potential customer cannot flick through the rail. For those with a mathematical turn of mind it has been calculated that you should try to display two items per square foot of area. So if your shop is 500 square feet you should aim to display 1,000 garments.

Standard shop fittings are surprisingly expensive. You can either try to get some surplus to requirement, when another shop is being re-fitted, or you can with the aid of a carpenter devise your own fittings. Remember that the rails will carry a lot of weight, and if fixed into the walls may, in use, come adrift. The rails should have some form of support to distribute the weight. For the same reason rails should not have too long a span. It is also easier for the customer to flick through a short rail, which features one type of merchandise, rather than tackling a very long, and more daunting rail.

A very thick wooden pole can be used as a rail from which to hang garments. To enable the hangers to move freely on the pole it should be waxed or varnished (waxing is easier to maintain). A cheap hanging system, much less expensive than shop fittings, would be a series of dividers, at right angles to the wall, with a ladder of slots into which thick wooden poles could be dropped. The ladder means the pole could be lowered or raised, depending on the required heights. If all the walls of the shop

A DISPLAY CHECKLIST

Outside

- ☐ Is the window clean?

- ☐ Are signs in the window straight, and accurate? (remove out of date information or tattered posters).

- ☐ Is the ledge (if any) at the bottom of the window and round the door clean and dusted?

- ☐ Is the window display neat, and items correctly and clearly priced?

- ☐ If there is an 'A' board sign, is it in good condition and correctly placed?

- ☐ Is the window well lit?

On Entry

- ☐ Is the doormat clean?

- ☐ What is the first impression of the shop? Is it clean, tidy, welcoming?

- ☐ Is the carpet, or floor covering clean?

- ☐ Are the shelves and fitments dusty?

- ☐ Is stock neatly displayed?

- ☐ Are all items properly hung, with hangers facing the same way, and labels showing?

- ☐ Is stock too jammed in to make it accessible?

- ☐ Is there a range of garments, and a good selection of sizes?

- ☐ Are the best selling categories given enough space?

- ☐ Is the till area neat and clutter-free?

- ☐ Are aisles clear, and all parts of the display accessible?

- ☐ Is the customer drawn to the back of the shop?

- ☐ Do any light bulbs need replacing?

- ☐ Are there trailing flexes, or other safety hazards?

- ☐ Has the layout and display inside the shop been changed recently? At least within the month.

were divided in this way within this system you can decide whether to have rails or leave open space, for example, in which to place a mirror, or have shelves or have large signs.

Using natural wood has an advantage over laminated finishes on chipboard, of which most shop fittings seem to be made, because it will not chip. To keep the wood surface clean, if they are likely to get a lot of finger-marks on them, varnish the surfaces (or scrub with soapy water with diluted bleach in it).

As well as fitments along the wall you may have enough space for fitments in the centre of the shop. Central units may be carousels that spiral downwards, on which half length garments can be hung or tables (with or without storage space underneath) on which clothes can be folded or bric a brac displayed. If you use tables you may need something to build up the height of the display not to eye level, as that would block out the view of the back of the shop and provide a screen for shop-lifters, but to chest height.

The accepted wisdom in charity shop management is 'if you can hang it up do so', but quilts, blankets, bedcovers and curtains are bulky when hung, and if you have enough, can make a good display when folded. For items that are not going to be hung, it will be easier to keep tidy if they are contained, either on shelves, or in boxes. For small items use the wooden packing boxes discarded by wine merchants (these should be sanded, and can be used as they are, or varnished or sprayed with paint).

Empty tea chests are too full of splinters, sharp metal corners and rather too deep to be useful as shop fittings - but look out for sturdy crates which have been used to ship in ceramics that are being discarded by cookery ware shops, which can be useful in a low cost display. Wicker washing baskets and vegetable display baskets make inexpensive shop fittings. (They may need replacing every three or four years depending on wear and tear.)

Ingenuity will produce a more interesting, welcoming and appropriately fitted out shop than any designed by a shop fitting company. It is not unusual for charities to spend £25,000 on shop fittings (including re-wiring, flooring and lighting). You need to sell a lot of second hand jumpers to recoup the cost. You could almost certainly reduce the cost by a third, if not half, if you do not use standard shop fittings or shop fitters, but employ a carpenter and electrician directly. Shop fitters work very quickly, often re-fitting a shop over a weekend - but they charge a premium for the speed of their service. It is very difficult to re-fit a chain of shops very quickly other than by using a firm of shop fitters, working to a formula.

There was a demand amongst those setting chains of charity shops in the 1990s (many of whom were drawn from conventional retailing) to standardise the shop and make them more like other retailers. They wanted charity shops to be brought more within the conventional retailing sphere, both in looks and management style. As a consequence the charity shops have lost a great deal of their individuality, and more seriously perhaps, have lost a place in public affections; they make the charities seem rich and powerful, rather than weak and in need of help.

Whatever your shop fittings try to give most display space to your best selling items. For example, if you sell more ladies separates than any other category of goods, try to put more of them out on display, than say men's

> **DO NOT** have your display space determined by the amount of stock you have donated, but rather by what sells.

suits. You may have dozens of pairs of men's shoes given to you, but sell very few, so do not take up precious display space by putting them all out. The only exception to this of proportional space is where an item will add interest to the display - for example a ball gown or page boy suit.

You will not be able to work out what categories will be the best sellers until you have opened your shop, so you have to be prepared to change your display in the light of your experience. It is also important to keep changing your display, to maintain customer interest. They will be tempted to revisit the shop if it looks as if there is a lot of new stock. Changing the displays and the position of the stock will emphasize this. New fixtures are not called for, just a re-arrangement of the stock on them.

The stock should be hung on appropriate size hangers. Do not use wire hangers, as they distort in use, and do not show the clothes to advantage. Try to use the same type of hanger for each type of garment. [Hang a sign in the sorting area showing the correct type of hanger for each garment, and the way the items should be hung from them.] Hangers should be facing the same way, with price ticket showing size and price, week number and a mission statement about the charity's work hung on the sleeve, or waist, so it can be easily read by a customer rather than having to rummage in the neck. Do not make the tickets too small to be legible for those without 20/20 vision. To attach the price ticket use small safety pins, or a punch tagger.

It makes sense to display stock by category, for example, ladies blouses or dresses or men's suits, and within each category to arrange it by size, starting with the smallest sizes and working along to the largest, from left to right. Put a size cube on each hanger, using a colour coded system. If you can find enough different colours of cubes you could also differentiate by category. Not only will the customer be able to see the sizes easily, but the shop staff will be able to see by glancing at the rails which sizes need topping up, so know what stock to bring forward from the stock room. Collecting the sizing cubes at the cash desk will provide a useful check on the impressionistic approach. There should be a large bin at the cash desk to collect hangers and a box or jar in which the days collection of sizing cubes can be dropped after each sale.

Putting the stock on the correct hangers, putting on size cubes and writing out a ticket and attaching it to the garment is the job of the sorter, working in the back-room, but it is the job of the shop staff, those serving on the shop floor, to see that the stock is correctly hung, in the right section, and the label still on it!

Make sure that all fittings and stock are easy to clean. The importance of housekeeping cannot be exaggerated. A shop that is dusty and dirty, gives the message that the stock is worthless, so why should anyone want to buy it? A dirty, poorly maintained shop attracts scruffy, poor quality donated goods and can only charge low prices for its goods. Once you let housekeeping standards drop it is very difficult to re-establish them. The shop should start clean and tidy and stay clean and tidy. Every person working in the shop shares responsibility for its cleanliness. It must not be a chore saved up for the lowliest volunteer. Shop managers should set the example by being willing to join in the cleaning. If the shop is in a terrible state and needs a real spring clean, consider closing for a day, calling in all the volunteers and really sorting everything out (this might include a quick coat of paint over the dirtiest surfaces). Once the shop is clean it is easier to keep it that way.

> **THE IMPORTANCE OF KEEPING THE SHOP CLEAN** cannot be over emphasised. A dirty shop deters customers and drags down the value of the stock.

THE STOCK ROOM

An essential part of the charity shop is the stock room, which has been described as its engine room. Because stock is not selected and bought from the suppliers, as in a conventional shop, but is donated, you cannot control the inflow of the stock. Your stock room becomes a manufacturing unit into which the raw material is delivered, and going through the process of sorting, brushing down and labelling, is transformed into saleable items.

All donated items should be gratefully and graciously received, then taken to be sorted out in the stock room. Not all the goods you receive are in fact saleable. To sell £1000 worth of goods you probably process £2,500 worth of goods which are later discarded. A further substantial quantity are not even priced and displayed. Everything has to be sorted, so its destiny can be determined!

The stock room should be clean, bright, and well ventilated and heated, because a great deal of time will be spent there. There should be a packing table (at counter height) on which each garment can be laid out, and checked for saleability, measured and labelled. It is best to have a counter height table, as the job is best done standing, as it involves moving round, taking incoming unsorted stock and putting it into one or other designated area. If your staff are elderly, and are not able to stand they should be provided with counter stools (but take care that they are stable).

There should be racks on which stock ready to go on display should be hung by category so it can be easily picked up and put on display in the shop. Goods which are not of merchantable quality - for example, torn, with cigarette burns, badly worn, faded - should be discarded.

The store room should be arranged so there is a conveyor belt system. Goods in - sorted - into racks by category for putting on display or into bags for collection by the rag merchants. It is important to keep the stock room tidy, and avoid any bottle-necks.

Once the store room gets into a muddle it is very difficult to tidy up. The messy stock room about which the supervisor or volunteer proudly says "It looks a mess but I know where everything is!" is a really bad idea, because everything grinds to a halt if she is ill or on holiday. No one works well in a mess. A great deal of time is wasted looking for things, hidden under piles of clothes. You should be able to see at a glance how the stock room is organised.

Keeping the stock room neat is important to prevent theft of stock by staff.

Not only does this make it possible for any staff member to use the stock room, but also reduces the opportunity for theft. (A very usual trick for theft from the stock is to sort incoming goods, and secrete the best items in bags tucked under other stock, to be removed when no one else is looking.) A really neat, clear, stock room removes the opportunity.

If the stock is a jumble of clothing, it encourages people to feel it is alright to help themselves rationalising that they are unwanted goods, with no value that "won't be missed". Although the stock of the charity shop has not been paid for, since it is all donated, does not mean it has no value. The tidy, well stock room gives the clear message to staff whether voluntary or paid, that the goods donated to the charity are wanted and needed, and should be accounted for as assets of the charity. If the incoming stock is treated with respect , and that includes how it is treated behind the scenes in the stock room, then it is likely to command a greater price.

As well as the sorting table, there should be frames into which heavy duty plastic bags are suspended, held open to receive discarded goods, to avoid fumbling about to open the neck of the bag every time you want to put something in it. Depending on your prior arrangement with the rag merchant you will need to sort discards into categories. Have a black sack for each category.

The stock room should be a secure area. If there is a back door from the stock room, say to a delivery bay or car park, make sure no one can slip in or out unobserved. Simple devices such as a shop bell over the door help alert staff to any unexpected to-ings and fro-ings which may mean an intruder or a helper removing sacks of the most desirable goods. Most of the stock is of relatively low value, so it is the persistent large scale removal of goods perhaps for re-sale elsewhere, which is the biggest problem. Exits from the shop, front and back should make it hard to remove large bags of goods without being observed.

3
STAFF

How many staff will you need

Organising a shift system

Paid staff or volunteers

Area and regional managers

Statement of employment

Payment of volunteers

Motivating staff and team building

Training

Health and Safety Regulations
- electricity regulations
- hazardous substances
- first aid
- fire
- disposal of waste
- safe manual handling

STAFF

Staff, paid or unpaid, are both the biggest problem and the biggest asset of any shop. The calibre of the staff is the main single factor in determining the success or failure of an individual shop. Good staff will overcome the drawbacks of poor location just as bad staff will negate its advantage. Good staff will be able to identify and overcome problems, bad staff will sink into a slough of despondency, and any problems will be exacerbated. Since the staff are the key factor, attracting, retaining and motivating staff should be given high priority.

From the outset you have to consider a number of questions. How many staff do you need? What tasks will need to be done, and can you expect one person to be able to do them all, or will you need more than one person? What are the particular qualities that you expect of your shop staff? What are you offering in return - is it just money, or can you offer training, work experience, interest, variety and companionship. Do you expect your staff to have a total commitment to your cause, or is it more important to you for them to be able to work the till?

Think about what you want and expect from staff before you recruit, because it is not fair to take on staff, volunteer or paid, and decide you do not like them, or they are not what you wanted, if you have not made clear what you did want. "I know what I like when I see it", may be, just about, alright as a policy on modern art, but it is not an acceptable attitude in recruiting staff. Too often those choosing staff do not think through what they want, what the job requires, or what personality type will fit in as part of the team.

> **THE CALIBRE OF STAFF** is the key factor in determining the success of any charity shop. Therefore the greatest care should go into finding and keeping the right staff.

HOW MANY STAFF WILL YOU NEED

Charity shops will have more staff, if they can get them, than an ordinary shop. There are three main reasons for this. Firstly, a large proportion of the staff will be volunteers, so the charity can afford a higher level of staffing. Secondly, because the donated stock has to be sorted and priced, there is a staffing need which a conventional retailer does not have. Thirdly, many of the volunteers are elderly so cannot work with as much physical energy as younger sales assistants.

Depending on the size of the shop and the level of trade, you should probably work on the basis of a team of four staff in the shop at any one time. This allows for two on the shop floor and two sorting and pricing. It may be useful to have another person on the shop floor, or bringing stock forward from the sorting area.

Do not overwhelm the supervisor with too many volunteers. Four staff is not a magic number, and the need in each shop varies. Some charities limit the number of shifts. They allow any volunteer to work to two four hour sessions a week.

Many shops will have a total of forty to fifty helpers. This, of course, represents a formidable task of supervision. Each session should have a 'team leader' whose job is to see the staff are kept happy and the shop well run. Where there is a full-time paid manageress there are usually fewer staff, and the manageress will take on the tasks of the session leader.

KEEP A BALANCE BETWEEN HAVING ENOUGH HELPERS AND TOO MANY

Too few mean:

- shop security cannot be maintained
- shop cannot be kept tidy and clean
- donated goods cannot be properly sorted and accumulate

Too many mean:

- a dreadful strain on management
- lead to squabbles
- staff get bored
- staff talk to each other rather than attending to customers

---

ORGANISING A SHIFT SYSTEM

Unlike conventional shops, charity shops nearly all operate a shift system. Most divide the day into two four hour shifts. Many prefer a two hour shift system, and this is particularly good for elderly volunteers.

ORGANISE THE DAY INTO SHIFTS

Limit the number of shifts a volunteer can work so:

- they do not get over-tired
- they do not get bored

The advantage of a shift system is that the staff, voluntary or paid, all stay fresh and enthusiastic. They do not get bored or over-tired. A full day in a shop, standing behind a till, or working at a sorting table, is physically demanding and it is better for people to go home before they get tired. Volunteers will be keener to return if they do not find the work exhausting.

Often there will be periods when there are few customers, so limiting the length of time any one member of staff is in the shop reduces the chance of boredom, and again this increases the chance of them returning.

Having different 'teams' of staff on a rota basis also overcomes a problem peculiar to charity shops, particularly those with volunteer staff, that those running the shop become very 'cliquey'. They are having such a lovely time playing at shop, and enjoying each other's company - that they start seeing the customer, or any other newcomers who volunteer, as the enemy. They are not welcoming, they are off-putting to customers, potential donors and helpers. Restricting the hours of volunteers in a charity shop also prevents over-dependence on the shop as a source of companionship and activity. It is easier to have a rule restricting hours that is uniformly applied rather than trying to impose it to deal with for example, an increasingly frail helper who has worked in the shop for years, to the exclusion of all other activities.

For many people the fact that they do not have to work a full week is very important. It enables people to volunteer, whilst a full-time job would be impossible for them to fit in with their other commitments. Half a day volunteering in a charity shop may provide just the right level of activity and stimulation for a retired person, or fit in well with a young mothers child-minding commitments. If you make working one or two sessions the norm then these people will feel able to work as equal members of the team.

> **KEEP A LIST OF PEOPLE** who will be able to help out in an emergency. Keep the list near the till.

If a session is too long, and someone has, for example, to collect children from school, then this should be incorporated into the time-table by mutual agreement. The advantage of a session system is that it allows flexibility, and can use a large number of very part-time staff. It is surprising how in the hands of the bossy, headmistress types it can be used to exclude people, because they cannot adhere exactly to the sessional times. How a supervisor uses the session system is a very good indicator of their management skills and suitability for the job.

Try to build up a team of people who will help out in an emergency. If you divide your week into twelve sessions, that is twelve half days, you will need a minimum of three teams, each responsible for four sessions. Encourage the team leader to build up a pool of people in the team who will help out occasionally, for example, when someone is ill or goes on holiday. Make sure the team leader trains a deputy within her team who can cover if necessary.

People will not turn out in an emergency if their previous experience of working in the shop is hanging about, making a desultory cup of coffee, and straightening a few rails. They will not judge it to be an emergency if they have not had enough to do, so make sure there is enough to keep them busy. There is nothing more irritating than responding to a call for help, at some sacrifice of free time or at the expense of a much more interesting activity, to find one's presence was not really needed.

The basic immutable rule is that if you are asking people to volunteer you must not waste their time. Of course, you cannot guarantee them customers, and most understand this quite well, but you do not need six people standing round waiting for custom when three or four would suffice.

Not all staff are needed at the same time. It may be that two people would open up and be in the shop for the first hour and a half, but two more are needed to cope with the late morning rush. The till roll at the end of the day will usually give a breakdown of when sales have been made, and it is worth analysing the information to see if it follows a pattern, and if you can refine your staffing to fit in with the busy periods. You may need more people over the lunch hour period, so have the morning and afternoon session overlapping to give that extra cover.

Whether the shop is run by a full-time manageress or a part-time supervisor, and whether the staff are paid or voluntary it is absolutely vital that everyone understands the need for punctuality and reliability. Anyone who cannot be relied upon should be spoken to, given a second or third chance and then asked to leave.

PAID STAFF OR VOLUNTEERS

A distinctive feature of charity shops is their dependence on voluntary, unpaid staff. Some are staffed only by volunteers, in others there will be a paid manager or supervisor, supported by volunteers. Relatively few charity shops have a wholly paid staff. Even though there has been a trend towards having paid shop managers, particularly for some of the fast growing chains of charity shops developed by the large national charities, for many paying staff in their shops would be an anathema.

How do charities decide whether to try to recruit volunteers or paid staff? There are advantages and disadvantages of both paid and unpaid staff. A big advantage of volunteers is they are cheaper. The saving to the charity boosts the shop's profitability. Indeed, without volunteer staff many charity shops would not make a profit. The profit in many equates with the value of the donated labour. Employing volunteers is not free, as out of pocket expenses such as travel should be refunded, and there is a higher cost of recruitment because turnover in volunteers is likely to be higher than of paid staff. This also means greater input in induction training and supervision.

Staff in charity shops are not actually very highly paid, indeed some charities recognising that the pay would not even approach an adequate minimum wage level, call the pay 'an honourarium'. One London based chain of charity shops, selling a larger than usual proportion of bought in goods, was paying £14,000 - 16,000 for its shop managers in 1993, which was higher than comparable wages in the retail sector for shops with twice the turnover. This charity also paid part-time shop assistants on a higher hourly basis than most department stores. Few charity shops are such generous employers. Shop managers pay of £8 - 9,000 seems more usual, and this falls drastically in areas of high unemployment.

VOLUNTEERS

ADVANTAGES OF VOLUNTEERS:

- saves money
- flexibility often attracts high calibre staff
- can get better qualified staff than if paying
- highly motivated

DISADVANTAGES OF VOLUNTEERS:

- need higher level of supervision
- need more (work shorter hours)
- staff turnover is greater
- often elderly, and lack physical stamina

When offering paid employment you are competing with other employers, who may not only be offering higher pay, but also more scope for promotion, and more congenial and varied work. Volunteers however, perhaps because they cannot work full-time because family commitments or lack of physical stamina, or inability to find paid work commensurate with their qualifications, may be prepared to work as part-time volunteers in jobs they would not consider as paid jobs. We are all familiar with the stereotype of the middle-aged, middle class professional wife who takes her voluntary work very seriously, and whilst it is a stereotype that does not truly reflect the variety of types of volunteers, and their changing socio-economic profile, it does enable one to understand that there is a pool of exceptionally talented people who one can attract as volunteers.

The disadvantages of relying on volunteer staff are that they will probably be a higher turnover in staff, as their circumstances change. Volunteers in charity shops are generally elderly (in many cases the average age of the volunteers is over 70!) and their physical ability to continue may decline, even when they will work on beyond their capacity. [One charity shop installed chair lifts and grip rails for its volunteers - a kindly gesture, but perhaps a rather sentimental one - as a more appropriate response might have been to recruit younger volunteers.] For housewives with young children volunteering in a charity is something to do which fits in with their commitments at a certain time in their lives. As the children grow up they can go out to work in paid jobs. Unemployed people may volunteer on their doctor's advice "to get out and meet people" as an antidote to depression or as a response to bereavement. They may not enjoy the work, nor find that the solution to their problems lies in working in a charity shop. Their stay will be short-lived, and may be disruptive.

A problem for any charity recruiting volunteers is how to reject unsuitable applicants. Often at vulnerable periods in their lives, needing a great deal of care and support, people volunteer for work in the shop, but they may be quite unsuitable. They may be too nervous, too obviously troubled to cope with the relatively high levels of social skills needed to get along with customers and co-workers. Whilst charities above all should take a lead in helping the disabled or disadvantaged achieve their potential, it will not help the shop's profitability if the customers avoid the shop because they are scared of the staff. There is a delicate balance between overcoming prejudices and destroying your business.

A CODE OF BEHAVIOUR

All staff, paid or unpaid, must be:

- punctual
- neat & tidy
- polite
- non-sexist
- non-racist
- honest

The prime aim of the charity shop is to raise funds for its cause. The opportunity to provide worthwhile, meaningful work for volunteers is an important by-product. But it is only a by-product, not the main aim, and this must be realised. Running charity shops, because they sell donated goods and have unpaid staff, is not playing at shop-keeping, it is a serious business. The need for the charity shop to generate profit is greater than for ordinary shops because failure to raise funds means suffering for the charity's beneficiaries, whether they are drought stricken families in Africa, or street children in Latin America or cancer patients in Abroath.

Whether staff are voluntary or paid you have to let them know exactly what you expect of them, and what standards and codes of behaviour are required. Behaviour unacceptable in paid staff is not acceptable because it is done by unpaid staff. For example, poor time keeping, untidy appearance, rudeness, racist or sexist behaviour would be reasons for 'dismissing' volunteers. You may want to give a first warning, and should have established and known procedures (see below) but you must make clear to everyone working in your shops that being a volunteer is not an excuse for bad conduct. If you treat your volunteers in a business like but friendly way at the time of interviewing and inducting them it will help to reinforce the message that standards of behaviour are expected to be high. Because people are not paid does not mean that they are not serious, and do not have to be treated as seriously. Oxfam advertises its shop manager jobs in local newspapers in the same way that other retailers would advertise for a manager. The advertisement is as large, as well set out and as carefully worded as any for a paid job. This shows that the fact it is not paid is incidental. The emphasis is on the work not its voluntary nature, and this is exactly how it should be.

Before you recruit staff think about what work you need done, and what sort of person will be able to do it. For example, do you want someone who will obey instructions or work to a scheme decided by management. Are you looking for someone who wants to be able to use a great deal of initiative? Would they resent close supervision? Is the ability to work with other people, and charm volunteers sufficiently important that it would over-ride an inability to cope with figures? How important do you consider past experience, or do you prefer to train your own staff? Is interest and commitment to the charity and its objectives important, or are you more concerned with retailing experience?

When recruiting paid staff one may be looking for someone who can undertake a range of the necessary tasks, from window

Working for a Fairer World
need a
VOLUNTEER ELECTRICIAN
with City & Guilds or equivalent qualification in their
KILBURN SHOP
to test and clean electricals, on Mondays and/or Tuesdays and/or Saturdays.
Please phone Marco Costa at the Kilburn Shop 071 624 6697 or West End Lane shop 071 435 8628.

Minimum commitment required is four hours a week.

OXFAM is striving to be an Equal Opportunities organisation and welcomes applications from all sections of the community.

Working for a Fairer World
WOOD GREEN
require a
VOLUNTEER SHOP MANAGER
This is an excellent opportunity to combine an interest in the Third World with the development of retail management skills.

We are looking for an enthusiastic and versatile volunteer to lead and co-ordinate the shop team in Wood Green, in order to achieve income targets.

Although desirable, previous experience is not essential as full training will be given.

Please call **081-446 4817** for an application form.

The closing date for applications is 22nd September.

OXFAM is striving to be an Equal Opportunities organisation and welcomes applications from all sections of the community.

dressing, through to keeping the accounts. In volunteers you can perhaps use people who have only one of the skills needed to help run the shop - perhaps sorting donated goods, or serving customers or writing price tickets. Do not find jobs just to keep volunteers occupied. You are not running an occupational therapy unit. But do have a flexible approach, and be adaptable in using the talents of your volunteer in a cost effective way.

AREA AND REGIONAL MANAGERS

It is calculated that once a chain of shops reaches eight shops there will be a need for an overall supervisor or area manager to keep a weather eye on them. In fact an area manager, can usually oversee about twelve shops, though they may feel overstretched at that level. Oxfam district retail managers supervise around twelve shops each, and British Heart Foundation area managers oversee between twelve and fourteen, and this appears to be the norm for the industry.

If an area manager is setting up new shops then the number she can effectively supervise is reduced. Also, where shops have paid managers the need for supervision is somewhat reduced. The number of shops that can be properly supervised will depend on geographical location. If the area or regional manager has to cover a very large area, she may in fact spend most of her time driving between shops, and relatively little time in the actual shops.

AREA AND REGIONAL MANAGERS have to see that the shops are run in accordance with the procedures set out by the charity and that the desired standards are maintained.

Each shop will have a financial target and it is the job of the area manager to work with the individual shop managers to see the targets are achieved. The area manager can compare each shop, and can see if one is more welcoming, or better displayed than the other. She can make judgements as to why one shop is managing to attract a large quantity of donated stock, whereas others may get very little. The shop which does the best sets the standard for the others, although, of course, the variations in size and location have to be taken into account.

All supervisory staff have an important function in preventing theft by staff, either of stock or cash. On visits to the shop, which should not be prearranged, but rather be unexpected, the till should be spot checked (the till roll and takings reconciled) and the stock room and shop inspected for any irregularities. Because they can compare the performance of shops in attracting donated goods, and levels of sales and donations, the area manager and in turn the regional managers are likely to be alerted to any shortfalls.

Charities with very large chains of shops will have not just area or district managers, each overseeing eight to twelve shops, but each area manager will be answerable to a regional director, who may oversee ten or twelve area managers. There may be ten or twelve regional directors who are answerable to head office management.

**TYPICAL STRUCTURE OF
NATIONAL CHARITY SHOP CHAIN**

Headquarter staff provide support
also direction to
▼
10 to 12 Regional Directors each oversee
▼
10 to 12 Area Managers
each oversee 8 to 14 shops
▼
Shop Managers

All charities running charity shops find, from time to time, that keeping control over the shops and the area and regional managers is difficult. It is made particularly difficult because of the peripatetic nature of area and regional managers' jobs. They are not based at headquarters but generally work from home, and spend most of their time on the road, visiting shops. It is therefore difficult to make sure they imbibe the ethos of the charity, as they would if they were at head office. Because they are out in the field they often feel they are the true torch-bearers for the charity's work, and the head office staff are not in touch with the grass roots of the organisation. This may be true, but since the head office staff are often concerned with updating the image of the charity, and modernising practises, it is very usual for friction to emerge, and for the area managers to resist rather than implement the changes required by top management. This resistance is transmitted to the shops, and makes it very difficult to create the cohesion, mutual respect and sense of common purpose that everyone would agree is desirable in any organisation.

The head office may have problems controlling the regional and area managers, but the area managers have similar problems controlling the shop supervisors. It takes great tact, friendliness and warmth to be a good area manager. The shop supervisor will resent an outsider who visits and criticises. The first duty of the area manager is to listen to the grievances and problems of those working in the shops. Grumbling should not be encouraged, but rather problems identified and suggestions as to possible solutions invited. The area manager is in the unique position of being able to bring forward solutions which have been tried and succeeded in other shops. A good area manager will always find something to praise when visiting a shop (if only the neatness of the staff's appearance). It is very easy for hostility to develop between the shop's staff and the area and regional supervisor, which in turn develops into resentment with head office. Shop staff can easily be made to feel their efforts are unrecognised and undervalued, if the area manager simply comes and points out all their short comings. Few people like to be criticised, or feel they need supervision, so the area manager has to work against the innate hostility. On the other hand, the interest of the business is not served if the area supervisors are so keen on not jeopardising their friendship with the shop staff that they avoid insisting on any improvements, and overlook bad practise.

SHOPS BUSINESS MANAGER
The South of England and Northern Ireland £20,541 plus car

SCF, one of the UK's largest charities, runs 156 shops selling donated clothing and a small gift range. ONe of three Shops Business Managers, this senior post is responsible for a staff team of 6 and 64 shops all staffed by volunteers.

You will be responsible for reviewing the performance of shops, identifying potential, and developing models of good practice - all to improve the bottom line results.

If you have at least 4 years experience of retail management in a fashion or charity chain; are able to manage staff at a distance, have good communication skills, are able to analyse financial data systematically while appreciating the role of volunteers, we would like to hear from you.

Shops Business Managers work from home, and you will need to be based in London or along the M4 corridor.

Closing date: 30th December 1993.

For an application form and job description please write to Maureen Muddell, Personnel Department, SCF, 17 Grove Lane, London SE5 8RD.

SCF aims to be an equal opportunities employer.

Save the Children

These problems arise in commercial businesses as well as in charity shops, but the problem is compounded in charity shops because if the image of the charity is damaged more is at risk than just the takings in the shop.

Generally, regional and area managers are paid employees. It may be possible to use volunteers, but the job involves a substantial amount of travel and this may be too physically taxing, and require too great a time commitment for a volunteer. When budgeting for regional or area managers allow for considerable travel and subsistence expenses, or every time a claim is made you will be unreasonably irritated, and this will mar the relationship. Agree at the time of the appointment the basis which repayment of travel costs is made (if it is per mile, or if all costs relating to the running of a car are met by the charity). Agree too, what subsistence costs are refundable. These are the sorts of issues over which enormous amounts of ill-will can mount up, so instead of both sides discussing ways of improving the shops, the atmosphere of resentment and grievance destroys the basis for amicable working.

The management of individual shops is generally done by a manageress who may be called the team leader, the shop supervisor or the manager. For many charity shops the manager will be unpaid, although there is a tendency to move to paid managers, though the rest of the staff are volunteers. Cynics might say that the amount that shop managers are paid means they are virtually volunteers. Few charities pay their shop managers at the salary levels of multiple retailers, because they could not afford to on the basis of the shop's turnover. Charities generally pay at the same level as small independent retailers in the same area. Because they do not want to be seen as paying below the minimum suggested wage levels, charities sometimes refer to their pay as an "honourarium" making clear that they recognise that the employee is worth more, but is working in part as a volunteer. Like all employers charities fix pay at the levels at which they can recruit staff. In the 1990s there has been fierce competition to be accepted as a volunteer in charity shops in areas of high unemployment.

WAYS TO FIND VOLUNTEERS

- word of mouth
- sign in the shop window
- card in the news agent
- local paper
- local Volunteer Bureau
- local companies
- local organisations

RECRUITING STAFF

Local shop staff can be recruited through the local press. Regional and National appointments may need to be advertised nationally. If placing an advertisement remember to give basic information, to avoid having to deal with a lot of inappropriate applications. You do not need to take a very large advertisement to attract attention. It gives the impression the charity has money to waste, and serious applicants will anyway look through all the job advertisements. Give a closing date for applicants, and plan how you are going to handle applications, including the criteria for selection. Some charities have been successful in simply putting a card in the shop window or in the window of the local newsagents.

To fill a paid job, it may be possible to promote from amongst the ranks of volunteers. It is right and proper that those that give up their time to help should have their commitment recognised and many charities make it clear that the best chance of getting a job with them is to work as a volunteer initially. There is an argument that all jobs should be advertised because that is fairer, and gives more equal opportunities to all sectors of the community. It is really up to the charity to decide its policy on advertising job vacancies. It is important that employment procedures including promotions as well as recruitment is perceived to be fair by those within and outside the organisation.

There are an enormous variety of ways to recruit volunteers. Cards in the windows of the shop, or local newsagents; advertisement in the local newspaper; letters to the editor of the local newspapers explaining some of the tasks for which you are seeking volunteers. Local Volunteer Bureau (which are usually listed in the Telephone Book, and can be found via the local Council of Voluntary Service) will circulate information on your needs, and act as brokers between volunteers and charities. Requests for volunteers can be sent to the Editor of the house journals of large local employers or to their personnel officer or to their journal for retirees. Local organisations, such as the churches or Women's Institute or community centre can all be approached for volunteers. Holding open days for recruitment at your charity shop, which you advertise in the local press and through posters in the shop window, give potential volunteers an opportunity to see if they like the work and have a look around, before they commit themselves. Word of mouth is important in recruiting volunteers, but should not be relied upon, lest it creates an atmosphere of cliquishness, where outsiders do not feel welcome. Surveys suggest that 50% of the population would volunteer if they were asked. Perhaps they might not all want to work in a charity shop, but some might.

ANYONE WORKING IN A CHARITY SHOP either as paid staff or a volunteer should provide two references. These should be checked by the charity.

When recruiting volunteers emphasise what you have to offer. You provide training in retailing, and the many tasks that are involved in running the shop, from working a till to keeping accounts, window dressing to dealing with customers. Working in the shop will not only provide an interesting activity, it also gives an opportunity to meet people and make new friends. It provides work experience, which will stand the volunteer in good stead when job hunting. Very importantly it enables the volunteer to help raise funds for the charity (a third of Oxfam's income is raised through its charity shops).

Join the team

'The individual here does have a voice in helping the individual in a totally different part of the world.'
Gill Bocock, Volunteer

DO YOU WANT TO MEET PEOPLE? Learn a skill? Have job satisfaction? Be part of a movement for change? Then join the Oxfam shops team.

Oxfam's 850 shops throughout the UK and Ireland bring in millions of pounds a year – almost one-third of Oxfam's income. Many of them are staffed entirely by volunteers, so the importance of shop helpers speaks for itself.

What you might be doing:

- pricing records and books
- designing a poster
- arranging a window display
- valuing collectors items – from postcards to porcelain
- driving to pick up donated goods
- sorting clothes for sale or recycling
- working on the till
- keeping accounts

On-the-job training is given a high priority.

Did you know that there are specialist Oxfam shops selling books, furniture, and crafts made by our overseas partners? And that unsold clothes are recycled by the Oxfam Wastesaver plant, the largest textile recycling plant in Europe?

Anyone working in the shop, in any capacity, should be asked to provide the names of two referees. If it is made clear that this is standard procedure, applied to everyone, and not being selectively used to imply distrust of the particular applicant, it should not give offence. The person conducting the interview should tell the applicant that two references will be needed, and then give a standard form, which can be filled in at the time or subsequently. This should explain the need for references in a informal manner, along the lines of "XYZ charity is delighted that you are applying to work (as a volunteer) in our XYZ charity shop. All those working for the charity are asked to provide the names of two people who know them well who can give references. They may be a neighbour, a friend, a former teacher or employer, but not a relative." The referees should always be contacted, initially in writing (enclosing a reply paid envelope). Describe the tasks involved in the job and ask if the applicant could, in the opinion of the referee, carry these out competently. Describe some of the qualities needed for the job - such as punctuality and ability to deal with customers and colleagues - and ask if the applicant has them. Ask specifically "Do you know anything that makes you think the applicant would not be honest in handling cash or stock?" Lastly, ask how long the referee has known the applicant, and in what capacity. You may want to follow up with a telephone call, either because they have not replied or because you want to double check, because people are more reticent in writing. You cannot be absolutely certain of the probity of all the staff, but you have a duty to be prudent.

STATEMENT OF EMPLOYMENT

Each person you recruit, whether they are volunteers or paid staff, should be given a 'job description' setting out what duties they could be asked to perform, and also setting out basic principles such as the expectation that they be punctual and that they do nothing to injure the good name of the charity. It should also detail their hours of work and any holiday entitlement. You may decide to list all the possible duties that could be expected and ask that the volunteer do some of them, or you may draw up each job specification separately (It may be easier to keep the job descriptions on a word processor and just slot in the appropriate sections).

It is essential that each member of staff, paid or volunteer, knows what is expected of them. The charity may issue in the form of a letter to the new recruit, a summary of the rules of the organisation. Try to be friendly and welcoming rather than strict and off-putting. Use friendly, familiar language rather than officialese.

The letter of appointment or job description (referred to by the Department of Employment as a Written Statement of Employment Particulars) should include details of types of activities necessary to run the shop, for example, serving customers; sorting and pricing stock and receiving donated goods; operating the till to 100% accuracy; keeping the shop clean and tidy; arranging and tidying stock; dealing with telephone enquiries and taking correct messages; carrying out cashing up and banking procedures to 100% accuracy; cleaning, ironing and mending stock as required; rotating and disposing of stock.

Codes of behaviour should be covered. For example, staff must be punctual. The shop must be opened and closed at the advertised times. Agreed administrative procedure must be followed. Colleagues and customers must be treated with courtesy and consideration. Confidentiality is expected. No racism and sexism will be tolerated. Staff are expected to know and be able to inform the public about the work of the charity, and how the money raised from the shops is spent. Staff must be in sympathy with the work and ethos of the organisation. It is the responsibility of the staff to familiarise themselves with Health and Safety Regulations and to do nothing to harm or put at risk themselves, the premises or their colleagues. Specify if any activities are regarded as obligatory - for example, any training sessions or induction courses. Is participation in special promotions compulsory?

Stipulate to whom the person is responsible, for example, if it is the shop supervisor and the area manager. They must also be told to whom they can complain, if they feel they have reason. Dismissal procedures should be laid

WRITTEN STATEMENT OF EMPLOYMENT

Must be provided to any paid staff within two months of starting the job.

THIS SHOULD SET OUT:

- what the job involves
- codes of behaviour
- to whom they are responsible
- disciplinary procedures

There is no legal obligation to give a written statement to volunteers.

VOLUNTEER JOB DESCRIPTION. It is advisable to give each volunteer some written information which details what they could be asked to do, and how the shop is organised, and where the stopcock is, and what to do in the event of a fire. Some charities provide sixty page booklets, others make do with two typed sheets.

down. When each person is given their 'job description' they should be asked to look at it, and feel free to raise any points that they are unhappy or confused about.

Both sides should sign the letter, to signify their agreement. The law requires that an employer provides a written statement of employment particulars, within two months of the job starting, for those working eight hours a week or more. More detailed information on the legal requirements are set out in the helpful Department of Employment leaflet PL700. It is not necessary to provide a letter of appointment to a volunteer but it is good practise.

PAYMENT OF VOLUNTEERS

It is estimated that a third of all volunteers are out of pocket because of their volunteering. This limits the ability to volunteer to those who can afford it, which is unacceptable on grounds of equality and more pragmatically rules out the legion of unemployed people who are full of energy and would make really good volunteers. Charities should all make a concerted effort to involve all kinds of people as volunteers, and to go out of their way to attract those who had not previously had any experience of volunteering. Considering the number of volunteers working in charity shops, ostensibly to raise funds for third world causes or the disabled, very few are from ethnic minorities, or the disabled. The only minority over-represented by charity volunteers is the elderly.

All volunteers should be offered expenses, regardless of whether they need them or not. In fact it is argued that best practise is to give all volunteers expenses. If a volunteer does not want to keep them, there should be a mechanism for re-donating them. It does seem somewhat cumbersome to have to work out all the different expenses, so they can be paid back, thus involving the charity in quite disproportionately large amounts of administration for relatively small sums of money. The argument is that to avoid any stigma attaching to volunteers who claim expenses it is better to pay all volunteers expenses. It is then up to each volunteer to decide whether to keep all or some or none of the money and give it back to the charity as a donation. This would not prevent other volunteers talking spitefully about the failure of colleagues to re-donate the expenses if they were so minded, in which case the whole point of the exercise would be lost.

It is right that volunteers should be offered expenses, and that it should be seen by everyone as appropriate. The reasons should be given by the manager at induction and re-iterated, and a phrase such as "we offer out of pocket expenses to everyone so we do not exclude anyone who might not otherwise feel able to volunteer. We do not always know about peoples' finances, and the demands on their income, so we offer expenses to everyone, as a matter of principle". Anyone making snide remarks about a colleague claiming expenses should be dealt with by the shop manager, then by the area supervisor, and told it is unacceptable, and if persisted in the person should be asked to leave.

What expenses charities reimburse varies. There is general agreement that it is proper to reimburse travel. It is not unknown for someone to volunteer in order to have a trip from the suburbs into town, and it may be prudent to fix a ceiling for travel expenses. Often lunch money up to an agreed amount will be paid. Some charities will offer to meet the cost of any care for dependents, but this is rare for charity shops. If protective clothing or uniform such as an overall is needed this should be paid for by the charity. Telephone calls or postage costs incurred by volunteers should also be reimbursed. The cost of using a car, for example for collecting donated goods, can be claimed, and the Inland Revenue issue mileage rates which they consider as not having an element of profit, and therefore not to be taxable.

The procedure for claiming expenses should be clearly stated when the volunteer is interviewed, and again at induction. If a volunteer does not seem to be claiming expenses the shop manager should check that it is not because they do not know how to do so.

DETAILS OF THE RULES OF PAYMENT OF EXPENSES FOR THOSE ON BENEFIT are given in a Department of Social Security leaflet "FB 26 Voluntary and Part-time workers."

The actual amount spent by the volunteer should be reimbursed rather than a flat-rate payment made and where possible receipts should be provided. Of course it is much easier for the charity if a flat-rate allowance is paid, because it cuts out the administration of dealing with individual claims, but this is not really possible as the Inland Revenue will treat any 'flat-rate' payments as taxable income.

Volunteers who are claiming 'benefit' should follow some basic rules, so as not to jeopardise their entitlement. Firstly, like all volunteers, payment of expenses should be for reimbursement of actual expenses, because any flat-rate payment will be treated as earnings, and benefit payments will be stopped accordingly. The volunteer who is claiming Unemployment Benefit should inform the local Benefits Agency that they are doing voluntary work. Because they have to be available for work (should any be offered) to qualify for Unemployment Benefit, volunteers whilst claiming Unemployment Benefit should warn the charity that they may have to go for an interview or take up work at 48 hours notice. The charity should not use this as an excuse for not taking on the volunteer, but be aware that this is a requirement of the DSS, not symptomatic of the volunteer's cavalier attitude.

Be careful not to jeopardise the volunteers' entitlement to benefits. You should be aware of the rules, and provide guidance to would-be volunteers. Do not allow volunteers who are claiming Unemployment Benefit to make a commitment to work full-time for an indefinite or specific period, for example, six months, because although you would like a commitment so you can plan, the volunteer could lose Unemployment Benefit, since they would not be available for work.

It is hard to believe but there have been cases where the Benefits Agency office have refused sickness and invalidity benefit to claimants who are doing voluntary work, on the grounds that if they are well enough to work in a charity shop they do not qualify. To protect themselves, those claiming sickness or invalidity benefits should be advised to get a letter from their doctor stating that volunteering would be of therapeutic value and check with their benefits office if their benefits will be affected.

The Volunteer Centre has an advisory service to which you can refer any queries on benefits or expenses and volunteering.

MOTIVATING STAFF AND TEAM BUILDING

People are not born knowing how to run a charity shop. They need to be shown both in general and specific terms how you want the shop to be run. Apart from the induction, there should be an ongoing training programme, used particularly to revitalise and inspire staff. It should include information on the work of the charity, and what happens to the money raised.

Not all charity shops have the same ethos, and all those working in the shop should be clear as to what is considered appropriate.

They should be encouraged to understand why a certain style of behaviour or organisation is chosen above another.

Staff will become demotivated if they are regarded as a 'lumpen' mass, who have to obey commands and have nothing to offer. There is nothing as valuable as the considered advice of those working on the shop floor. They can feed back information, and are the management's best researchers. They should be trained to watch out for trends, and to have enquiring minds. This is not the same as perpetually carping. Nor is there unlimited time to stand round and discuss what should be done. Many people prefer chattering to doing and will be glad of the new audience the area supervisor provides. Confronted with a member of staff who insists on holding forth endlessly, and stopping everyone getting on with work, formalise the procedure, set up a suggestions form, and ask them to put the suggestion in writing. This will concentrate their thoughts, and reduce the stream of consciousness flow! It requires tact.

The induction of staff, paid or voluntary, is very important in setting the tone. It is an opportunity to make clear what standards are expected, what tasks to be done, and the spirit in which that is to be carried out. The induction day is the opportunity to make clear what behaviour will not to be tolerated, and will lead to summary dismissal. This may include inappropriate or rude behaviour to customers or colleagues, including racial or sexual harassment.

Some of the causes for dismissal will be understood, such as stealing cash or stock, but others may come as a surprise, like giving discounts to staff or customers, or failing to keep to agreed procedures. Unreliability can be a reason for dismissal. It is much easier to list the things that will lead to people being asked to leave at the outset, because then in the event of difficulty the supervisor will be seen to be acting fairly, and in accordance with the rules. If there are no guidelines then it is awkward to have to introduce them.

The person giving the offence (except in cases of theft) rarely believes their conduct to be wrong or inappropriate. Having a set

TO GET THE BEST OUT OF STAFF

- keep them busy
- praise good performance
- motivate by keeping them informed on the charity's work
- show them other (better) shops as examples
- listen to their problems & suggestions

of rules makes it easier for the supervisor to raise the matter in the first place, and easier to carry through a disagreeable task by referring to her obligation to enforce the rules. It goes without saying that the matter should be handled as kindly and discreetly as possible. It is inappropriate to treat any miscreant working in a charity shop as an example to deter the others. There should be an appeal system, and this should be made known during the induction.

To get the best out of staff, particularly volunteers who do not have the incentive of remuneration, organise the shop in such a way that they feel that their time is well spent, and that they are needed. Standing, or sitting around doing nothing is dispiriting. People volunteer in order to feel needed and useful. Whilst you cannot supply customers, you can devise policies to attract customers and use your volunteers to implement them. Just keeping the shop tidy and well dusted is quite a rigorous day's work especially for a shop with a lot of passing motor traffic. Rarely is a shop in bad condition because the staff are too busy to keep it tidy. It is more likely that they feel too bored and demoralised to care.

People work better when praised than they do when scolded. Make sure the area manager, regional manager or anyone visiting from head office finds something nice to say about the shop, and tell them to say it before they make any critical remarks. It may be hard to find anything good to say - the window may be filthy and the displays a mess, the shop cluttered or littered with the stock and the sorting area a nightmare of black plastic bags and wire hangers. In that case try a compliment about how nice the staff look or even what a pretty colour their clothes are. Always try to reinforce any good behaviour by praising it.

The shop manager, or team leader, is critical in setting the standards for the shop. If she is lax it is difficult to motivate the rest of the staff. Apart from pointing out practical improvements that could be made, it may be helpful to take her to a good, well-run shop (part of your chain or some other charity's) and hope that the example will be helpful in persuading her to raise her standards.

If the shop is not run in the way and to the standard required the staff should be invited to discuss problems they have in carrying out their job, and it may be that by listening to their problems and working together to find practical solutions you can improve their morale and their performance. It is important that staff feel their efforts are recognised and valued. Allowing them to have a voice makes them feel valued. Take care that if inviting staff comments you actually listen to them, because if you do not it will exacerbate their frustration. If the staff merely complain and avoid all attempts at overcoming problems (what psychiatrists stigmatise as 'problem identifying/solution rejecting types') and if you find as a group working together they are reinforcing each other's sense of grievance, then try to split the team up. Identify the 'ring leaders' and haul them off for re-training, perhaps by taking them to another shop, or taking them to see something of the charity's work. Encourage discussion of problems and discourage complaining behind people's backs. Cultivating an open optimistic attitude is an important part of the induction training.

People like to work for the company it provides. This is particularly important for volunteers who do not have the incentive of wages to keep them loyal, so try to ensure that they are not isolated. Whilst you do not have to assume the role of a hostess giving a party, do consider the need for companionship when considering staffing and rotas.

To improve the common sense of purpose, now fashionably called team building, consider having monthly get-togethers for all those working at the shop, so they can exchange views, and iron out problems of changeover that might otherwise develop into causes for complaint within one shift. For example, if those working on Tuesday afternoon always find the stock sorting area a mess, instead of blaming the Tuesday morning shift of slatternly behaviour, they should raise the matter informally, and see if, in fact, the sorting area is always a mess, except after the tidy up on Tuesday afternoons. Or perhaps it will be discovered that the Thursday morning lot cause the mess and no-one has the energy to rectify it except the hard working Tuesday afternoon shift!

Keep the staff, paid or voluntary, all working for the same cause, and on the same side. It is very easy for feuds to develop between the different shifts, so whilst competition is healthy, and the friendly rivalry that makes them want to beat the Thursday afternoon team's takings can get the best out of them, it is not desirable for the energy that should go into running the shop to be deflected into a vendetta against co-workers!

All surveys show commitment to the cause is very important in motivating those working in charity shops. The British Heart Foundation even found it more important than paying commission on sales. The majority of those working in shops raising funds for medical charities have relatives who have suffered from the disease in question. The army of volunteers, who work in Oxfam shops, 26,000 of them are moved by the plight of the Third World, and have faith in Oxfam's capacity to help. It is very important that the shop staff are kept informed as to how the money they raise is spent, so that their enthusiasm for the work is sustained. Oxfam sends its long serving volunteers on visits to overseas projects. Other charities have open days, to which they ensure volunteers are invited. Remember, if you invite them treat them well. Make sure a senior member of staff or a trustee is briefed beforehand to thank them personally for their efforts, and comment on their achievements. The volunteer will thus be reassured that their work is known, and valued, and makes a difference.

If you treat your staff well, voluntary or paid, they will encourage their friends and family to come and buy in the shop. They will support your charity through donations and ultimately through legacies. Those who feel aggrieved or critical of the way the shop is run, will carry that hostility over to the charity and its work, and will broadcast it to anyone willing to listen. Research shows that those who have had good service in a shop tell no-one or one person, and those who have had cause for complaint tell, on average, nine people. Your charity needs people to hear good of it, and your shop staff should be seen as ambassadors.

TRAINING

All staff have to have some form of training. This can be an informal induction - "Here's the stock room. This is Grace, the supervisor, and this is how the till works" - or it can be formal, with courses and lectures, written examinations and a certificate at the end.

All staff should have an induction, this should be organised with a checklist to make sure it is done properly. They should be shown around the building, introduced to their colleagues; told where to keep their coats, where the lavatories are; how and where to make tea; what the rules are; what is expected of them and others. They should be shown any health and safety information, and told where the first aid box is, and what to do in the event of an accident. At induction give staff information on the charity's work, and make clear expected standards on race and equal opportunities.

If you are rather slap-happy over the induction process, staff may feel that sets the tone and you are quite casual about all aspects of work. First impressions count .

After the induction day, what training should you provide for your staff? Do you need to provide any? There are three main reasons for having ongoing training. The first is to increase the skill level of the staff, teaching specific skills, for example, on merchandising and display, which they could not simply learn on the job. Secondly, being prepared to invest in training can be a valuable way of telling people they are appreciated, that they are worth bothering with. Thirdly, training gives an opportunity to meet other people, with whom information on how to solve problems can be exchanged.

> ## THE ADVANTAGES OF STAFF TRAINING
>
> - teaches necessary skills
> - shows a 'professional' approach to work
> - improves staff motivation & morale
>
> ---
>
> ## DISADVANTAGES OF STAFF TRAINING
>
> - costs money & time
> - is seen by staff as a day out/off
> - can be used by staff for their own ambition, not for the organisation's benefit

Inevitably, some staff regard training as a punishment. Instead of welcoming the opportunity, they see it as a criticism of their abilities, and are insulted by the suggestion that they might need training. They arrive at training sessions cross and reluctant. When asked what they have got out of the course they usually say "I was made to come." Their attitude ensures they learn nothing, then feel their position vindicated.

There are a number of options for training staff and management of charity shops. In the larger organisations, training is often provided in-house. With literally thousands of staff in the shops it is clearly desirable to provide in-house training, to try to standardise performance. It is also more cost effective to train large numbers of people in-house. It also provides an opportunity for people to meet colleagues from different shops.

The disadvantage of training in-house is that the participants do not get a broader perspective, they do not meet people from other organisations who have other ways of dealing with problems. Outside training can bring fresh views. It may also be taken more seriously by participants.

Training specifically for those working in charity shops is organised by the Charities Advisory Trust, Radius Works, Back Lane, Hampstead, London, NW3 1HL. The Charities Advisory Trust also organise an annual conference on charity shops. More general training for those working in the voluntary sector is provided by the Directory of Social Change. The Charity Shops Group provides a forum for the sharing of ideas and information for those working in charity shops.

NATIONAL VOCATIONAL QUALIFICATION IN RETAILING: SPECIFICATION FOR LEVEL 1 showing what tasks a person should be capable of doing to perform their job successfully.

To gain a Level 1 Certificate, candidates must complete all Level 1 Foundation Units and at least two of the Level 1 Optional Units.

LEVEL 1 FOUNDATION

1   Providing a service to the Customer
2   Contributing to the maintenance of Health & Safety in the retail workplace
3   Contributing to good housekeeping routines
4   Maintaining relationships in the retail workplace
5   Contributing to the security of the retail workplace

LEVEL 1 OPTIONS

6   Handling Stock
7   Processing the sale
8   Achieving a sale
9   Maintaining Hygienic standards of food handling
10 Preparing goods/products to meet customer requirements
11 Treating or altering goods

These standards are drawn up by The Distributive Occupational Standards Council from whom detailed descriptions of what is covered can be obtained.

For those wanting to provide staff with the opportunity for a formal training programme, staff can work for National Vocational Qualifications, and National Vocational Qualifications in Retailing. National Vocational Qualifications in Retailing set out exactly the tasks that a person should be able to do to carry out their job effectively. There are four levels of qualifications. The advantage of National Vocational Qualifications is that they are the government backed vocational training, which is nationally recognised, so staff gaining a National Vocational Qualification can use it in applying for other jobs, as a standard qualification.

Some charity shop chains, such as Oxfam and Barnardo's provide staff with the opportunity to gain National Vocational Qualifications. To do so an organisation must have the infrastructure to be able to provide both the necessary training, the appropriate people to carry out the assessment and the administrative capacity to keep the necessary records. There is a cost, not only in staff time, both for trainers and trainees, but also to register as an approved centre with the Distributive Occupational Standards Council. There is a registration fee for each candidate, and a charge for the certificate.

It is attractive to staff to be able to get qualifications. It adds status and purpose to the job. From the employers point of view it is only worthwhile if the staff stay long enough for the investment to be realised. NVQ's provide a structure to the training, and a sense of progress in the job, which should lead to improvement almost immediately.

Level 1 is a basic level for sales assistants, it is reckoned that a new entrant should be able to tackle level 1 National Vocational Qualification after 3 months; level 2 is for a sales assistant with more responsibility, so could be paced for a year; level 3 is for skilled supervisory staff or departmental managers, and level 4 for a manager. When staff take levels 3 or 4 depends on their skill level on entry.

The tasks set out in the National Vocational Qualification Performance Criteria are a very useful training checklist. Even if an organisation feels unable to commit itself to providing National Vocational Qualification registered training, they should look at the retail standards, to give a useful guide to what should be expected of staff.

HEALTH AND SAFETY REGULATIONS

Charities, like other employers, have a legal obligation to observe the Health and Safety Regulations. It is not clear if volunteers have to be covered by Health and Safety Regulations, but it is certainly good practise. The old Health and Safety at Work Act has been replaced by European Community regulations. The employer has a moral obligation toward staff and public not to put them at risk. There is also a legal obligation, and the employer who fails to take due care, or train employees to take care, may be sued by anyone suffering as a result of that failure.

The main rules affecting charity shops are set out in six regulations:

- **Management regulations.** You must make a written assessment of risks at the workplace and keep your workforce informed of them. You have a duty to keep those at risk under surveillance.

- **Work equipment regulations.** There are strict rules, for example, on ventilation, window safety.

- **Workplace regulations.** Common sense prevails. One needs correct equipment, properly maintained. All staff should know how to use the equipment. Do not assume they know - show them.

- **Screen regulations.** There are strict regulations on the use of VDU screens.

- **Personal protective regulations.** Protective clothing should be worn where necessary. For example, masks, rubber gloves and overalls should be worn when sorting donated goods. They must be kept in good order.

- **Manual loads regulations.** Volunteers over fifty years should not lift bags/sacks weighing over ten kilogrammes. Staff should be given instructions on correct lifting procedures.

Full information is available from the Health and Safety Executive, and local Environmental Health Officers. (see resources section.)

ELECTRICITY REGULATIONS
All electrical goods must be inspected as frequently as possible, for example, plug sockets should be checked every eighteen months .

It may be safer to provide cordless kettles and irons, to reduce the chance of accidents caused by trailing cords.

HAZARDOUS SUBSTANCES
All staff must be able to identify toxic substances; know how they can be safely stored and handle the substances properly. Toxic substances include: washing up liquids, bleach, cleaning fluids and tippex!

FIRST AID
There should be a well stocked first aid box. Items such as paracetomol or lemsip should not be kept. That is a matter for the individual.

FIRE
There should be clearly marked fire exits. All staff (including volunteers) should take part in fire drills. The local fire brigade will inspect premises and advise on any necessary equipment, such as fire extinguishers and marking of exits.

It is helpful to have a Health and Safety notice board, showing basic information, for example, on lifting; on fire drill, or on which staff can list any allergies.

DISPOSAL OF WASTE

The local authority or a registered collector must be used and there must be a declaration as to what is being disposed of.

Introduction to the Health and Safety Regulations should be an important part of any induction programme. Give all staff and volunteers a check list on what to do in an accident or a fire. Tell them the hazards to look out for in the shop, and tell them the procedure to deal with the hazard.

Establish a 'responsibility' procedure that makes clear what is to be done when a hazard is discovered, for example, a tear in a carpet or a loose handrail. Keep an accident book, which should be checked by the supervisory staff - and acted upon. Discourage grumbling and encourage action. Make people take active care of themselves and their own safety.

Most Health and Safety Regulations are common sense. A difficulty for the employer is that they assume the employee exercises no common sense at all, and has to be protected from danger like a small child. For example, one would not normally expect to have to advise adults against drinking lavatory cleaner. However, one should remember that there are many accidents at work. In 1992, twenty nine million workdays were lost through back injuries caused through lifting.

Health and safety regulations protect those working in the shop, as well as customers visiting the shop premises.

Protection of customers from the potential hazards of any items they might buy, are covered by a myriad of laws and regulations. These are dealt with in the section complying with Trading Standards Legislation in the chapter on stock.

STAFF SHOULD KNOW WHAT TO DO

- in the event of fire
- in the event of an accident
- if someone is suddenly ill
- if someone has an epileptic fit
- if there is a burglary
- if there is a broken window
- if there is a flood (from plumbing or storm)
- if firedoors jam
- if chemicals (cleaning materials) spill

LIFTING

Practise these methods whether lifting a shopping bag or moving goods:

ONE PERSON LIFT
("squat lift")

1. THINK before doing anything.

2. STAND as close to the load as possible. Spread your feet to create a stable base (slide the load close if it's on a shelf).

3. BEND your knees and keep your back in a natural line. Don't bend your knees fully, as this will leave little power to lift.

4. GRASP the load firmly.

5. RAISE your head as you start to lift.

6. LIFT with your legs. Use your leverage, momentum, balance and timing for a smooth action. Move your feet.

7. HOLD the load close to the centre of your body.

4
STOCK

Bought in or donated goods

Selling donated goods

How to get donated stock

Sorting
- *complying with trading standards legislation*
- *sorting clothes*
- *pricing garments*

Sorting bric a brac

Disposing of unsold stock

STOCK

BOUGHT IN OR DONATED GOODS

Ask members of the public to describe a charity shop they will nearly all say it sells second hand clothes given to the charity. The first Oxfam shop was set up to sell the surplus of clothes donated to the charity for refugees overseas. Most charity shops sell clothes. They may also sell bric a brac, small items of furniture, furnishings, books, records, games, toys and jewellery. What they sell depends on the space available and what they are given to sell. A few charity shops which sell only books or records or furniture, these often have been built up as a result of the enthusiasm of an individual, who may have worked in one of the charity's ordinary shops and developed a specialist trade which they then expand to a fully fledged shop.

The majority of goods sold in a charity shop have to be donated if the charity is to qualify for the valuable tax concessions on charity trading. (Except for the few instances where charities are running shops as part of their primary purpose.) These concessions include exemption from tax on the profits: a massive 80% mandatory relief on the uniform business rates, with a further 20% at the discretion of the local authority; and the very favourable zero rate on VAT.

To qualify for these concessions the shop has to sell 'mainly' donated goods. 'Mainly' is a very vague term, and gives rise to a great deal of confusion in people's minds. The definition that matters is that given by the Inland Revenue and the local authority, they are the bodies which could withdraw the tax concessions. In fact there seem to be very few cases where the Inland Revenue have argued that the charity shop is selling too high a proportion of bought-in non-donated stock. The Inland Revenue are clear that mainly merely means more than half. There are often cases where local authorities have tried to refuse rate relief because the shop is selling what they regard as too high a level of bought in goods: a zealous public servant, half informed on the restriction of rate relief to donated goods, gets over excited and tries to withdraw mandatory rate relief. The local authority has had to back down, when the exact rules are pointed out to them.

Generally charities are very careful not to even approach a level of bought-in stock over which they could be challenged. 'Mainly' is taken by the Inland Revenue as more than half. To be on the safe side it is sensible to have more than a 55%/45% split. Some charities, and their advisers, fix on a 65:35 ratio, and some are so terrified of the rule and have so little understanding of it that they proscribe the sale of any bought in goods. When the Inland Revenue refer to 'mainly' they mean as a percentage of turn-over (i.e. sales income) not space in the shop taken up for displaying goods.

> **TO QUALIFY FOR TAX CONCESSIONS** a charity shop must be selling mainly or wholly donated goods. Mainly means more than half.

It might be that a charity buys in a few, high priced items, and though the quantity sold is very low compared to the number of donated goods, as a percentage of turnover it exceeds the sale of donated goods. If it happens once it may escape attention, but the charity should be aware of the implications if it buys in stock for re-sale. The situation can arise unwittingly, for example if a manufacturer offers goods at very low prices and the charity sells them at very high mark-up (for example, buying at 10p and selling at £5). The charity should arrange with the supplier to buy a few of the items at a higher price and be donated the others. (For example, instead of buying 1000 items at 10p the charity should buy 40 items at £2.50. The cost is still £100, but as proportion of turnover the sales of 40 items at £5 is £200, the remaining 960 @ £5 yield £4,800 which is for sale of donated goods.)

In some charity shops, there are clearly substantial quantities of new goods. The charities involved claim to take care to satisfy themselves that sales do not exceed half of turnover. Sometimes these include products made by the beneficiaries of the charity, for example blind or disabled workers in sheltered workshop, sales of which would be regarded as primary purpose trading, and so entitled to all the concessions on donated goods (except zero rating of VAT).

> **SELLING BOUGHT-IN GOODS** must be done through a trading subsidiary except where the turnover is so small that the de minimus rule would apply.

When goods are bought in for re-sale, this part of the operation should be run through a trading subsidiary, not by the charity, except if it is so small that it can be said to be covered by the de minimus rule. The charity should charge the trading subsidiary for the facility of selling its goods in the shop (but on the basis of actual costs rather than to make a profit, because the charity would otherwise become liable to tax on the profit). This applies not just to sales of bought in goods supplied by the trading subsidiary, but also where a trading subsidiary is running all the shops on behalf of the charity, because the goods are really donated to the charity, and the charity should charge for the use of its name.

Sales of bought-in goods are liable to VAT at the standard rate. They have to be accounted for separately on the VAT return, and in the shop's accounts. They should be rung up on the till using a different code from the sales of donated goods. Because they were bought, using charity funds, they have to be carefully accounted for, and a stock-take done at the very least for the annual audit.

Generally speaking, apart from the sale of Christmas cards and Oxfam's success with the sale of Bridge goods, which has objectives other than just profit, ventures in selling bought in goods have not always been a financial success. They often are embarked on with enthusiasm by staff who are bored or frustrated with the existing shop operation, or who have always wanted to run gift shops, and in fact they underestimate how difficult it is to combine the sale of donated, second hand goods, with the sale of new goods. Some charities have turned to new goods because they have found it increasingly difficult to attract donated goods. It is the sale of new goods which creates the opposition of small traders who feel the charity shops, with their tax concessions are competing unfairly. There is some evidence that charities are turning away from buying in stock for re-sale, having had their fingers burnt.

There is a certain logic to having bought-in goods. After all, the shop has a pool of supporters who may be prepared to buy, for example shampoo or stationery out of a sense of commitment to the cause. It makes good commercial sense to give customers an opportunity to 'add on' purchases, to increase the value of each sale. But trying to combine new and donated goods should be approached cautiously.

The atmosphere of the shop may be wrong. Customers may be in "the looking for a bargain" mode. They may want to buy new goods in a pleasant environment, say of a shopping mall or department store. The buyer for the charity may be unable to compete effectively with either the barrow boys, the huge multiples or the shops that buy up bankrupt or fire damaged stock. One over enthusiastic charity shops manager took to attending auction sales of bankrupt stock, and was jubilant at having bought hundreds of denim jackets at 50p each. However they failed to sell in the charity's shops, and the charity failed to recover its investment. Caution should always be exercised in the spending of charity funds, and they must not be used on speculative ventures. The essence of all expenditure of charity money is that it should be done with prudence.

SELLING DONATED GOODS

There are enormous advantages in selling donated goods, apart from the tax and rates concessions. The main advantage is, of course, that the stock is free. In fact it is not totally free because the charity will incur costs on attracting donated goods, on collection and on equipment costs in sorting and cleaning and preparing for sale. But these costs should be small compared with the costs of actually buying stock. This reduces the need for working capital, which is a great advantage for any charity and even more so when shops are run by a trading subsidiary.

In a conventional shop, the buying involves visits to trade fairs, or maintaining contacts with travelling salesmen, keeping abreast of new products and looking at the products offered by competitors. The actual placing of orders generates a substantial amount of paper work, checking of deliveries and payment of invoices. The shop selling donated goods is spared all this work. It is spared much of the trouble of stock control and stock taking (although it will not avoid it altogether in a properly run shop).

Donated stock means the shop has a constantly changing range of stock. There is a serendipity effect - the customer never quite knows what to expect, and often regular customers will visit a charity shop three or four times a week to make sure they do not miss any new exciting bargains! The fast changing nature of the stock and its wide variety, with scarcely any two items the same, enables a well run charity shop to keep up a momentum and retain customer interest in a way envied by conventional retailers, whose ability to change their stock depends on restrictions on space and capital. Generally a shop keeper can only introduce new lines to replace items sold. The charity shop can introduce new stock as long as it is donated.

ADVANTAGES OF DONATED STOCK

- low cost
- reduces need for working capital
- reduced administration
- constantly changing stock
- greater variety of stock

DISADVANTAGES

- cannot control stock availability
- dependent on donations
- may lack most popular sizes and colours
- get the goods at the wrong season

A charity shop cannot control the range of goods on offer. Goods cannot be re-ordered when they are sold, and it may simply happen that donations received in a particular week or fortnight may be almost all of size 8 short sleeved dresses, when what is needed is size 16 separates. A charity with a chain of charity shops may operate a central distribution system, so a shop low on certain sizes or types of clothing can draw on over-stock from other shops. It may be possible to operate such a scheme informally, with the area manager transferring goods from one shop to another in the back of his car. Some charities may use a central warehouse sorting operation (although extreme caution should be used in incurring the extra costs, since most of the donated goods in charity shops will in fact remain unsold, and be sold off to a waste merchant). One small charity shop chain ships overcoats from its London shops up to Durham, where new University students, unaware of the chills of the Geordie climate, arrive coatless in the autumn, so that the Durham shop does a brisk trade in overcoats. Make sure the cost of transporting the stock is recovered in the sales price. It is very easy to forget to attribute all costs.

In conventional retailing goods may be ordered to add interest to the window or range of goods. The charity shop cannot order in designs of a more lively colour or design to brighten up the display or add interest. But an astute shop manageress or area supervisor will set aside and introduce at intervals, any 'show stoppers'. Goods can be set aside for 'back to school' or 'Easter bonnet' or 'party wear special' promotions.

HOW TO GET DONATED STOCK

If the charity shop has to rely on what it is given, making sure it attracts the right quantity and quality of donated goods is essential. An estimated 3/4 million tons of used clothing is thrown away in household rubbish every year, so there is clearly a great deal of scope for charity collections. The main ways to attract donated goods are firstly, to have a shop where people know they can bring unwanted goods. The better the appearance of the shop the better the standard of donated goods it will attract. Most people will give to whichever shop is the most convenient. They are motivated less by the cause than by wanting not to throw things away, happy to find someone who wants it, and though they have to be generally sympathetic to the charity to whom they give the goods, the convenience of delivering to the shop is an over-riding factor. Committed supporters will collect and deliver

bags of goods into the shop. They simply need to be reminded from time to time that the shop needs more clothes, or accessories or books etc.

Make sure you display the opening hours on the shop door or window, so people can know when they can deliver in donated goods. Think about the shop hours. It may be that by opening for very short hours, say 11 till 4 Monday to Friday, you preclude anyone who works a full week being able to bring any goods into the shop. Bags of goods left in the shop entrance are a fire risk, a nuisance because they may encourage passers-by to break into the bags and take what they want, or simply annoy the neighbours because they feel it lowers the tone of the street. For some charities the bags of jumble could pose a security risk, by providing cover for fire bombs or other explosives.

Consider the feasibility of a 'bunker' for deliveries out of hours. It might not be possible or desirable for all but it could be worthwhile for some. You can place collection bins outside the shop, into which donated goods can be dropped when the shop is closed. Be aware of safety when constructing the bins - do not obstruct the pavement; be aware that blind people could walk into unexpected obstacles; take care no child could climb in and get trapped or suffocated. These 'clothes banks' can be, with the consent of the local authority, placed alongside the bottle banks and other recycling units, at garages or supermarket car parks. They can be specially labelled with the charity's name, logo and mission statement, and come in a variety of styles and sizes. Each charity has to judge whether the cost and the trouble of emptying them, is equal to the value of the goods collected and the publicity of having one's charity's name kept before the public.

People's preparedness to bring their donated goods into a charity shop depends on the warmth and sincerity of the thanks they receive. The stern shop manager who greets a donor with "Is it clean? We only want clean things" not only upsets the donor, but ensures they will never set foot in the shop again, and probably will never give anything to the charity including cash donations, a covenant or even a legacy! It is vital that people bringing donations of goods to the shop are properly thanked.

A really effectively run shop will train its staff, whether volunteer or paid, to be especially nice to people who donate.

They are highly valued customers just as surely as those who buy goods, because they are choosing the charity shop to give to. Try to keep the staff informed as to the ways in which the money the shop raises is being spent and to convey them to the donors. Try to give an example which gives a mental picture -

"Last year we raised enough to pay for a water supply and sanitation for a refugee camp in Africa"
"We bought bicycles for community health workers in India"
"We provided the funding for a research project at X University, which is helping to find a cure.."
"We sent two children on holiday to Kent"
"We bought equipment for a crèche and play group"

Give the person a feeling that their gift has made it possible. If you give your donors a warm glow they will give again, and speak of your cause warmly to their friends.

In an attempt to round up all available stock, many charities offer to collect. If volunteers are collecting then it is probably cost effective. Collecting by paid staff, in a van paid for by the charity, is not always cost effective because such a high proportion of the goods may not be saleable. You can try to increase the quality of the donated goods by advertising the fact you collect in prosperous areas but once you advertise the fact that you collect you cannot pick and choose for whom you will actually provide the service. As well as offering to collect you will almost certainly be asked to do so, both by telephone enquirers or people coming into the shop.

> **TREAT THOSE DONATING GOODS AS VALUED CUSTOMERS.** They are choosing your shop to bring goods to. Thank them warmly, regardless of what they bring.

You may want to inform undertakers, doctors or solicitors in your area that your charity will collect, since these are people whose advice may be sought when there is a death. Oxfam has launched a collection scheme with the British Association of Removers, where OXBOXES or OXBAGS are given to those moving house, to be handed over to Oxfam, a brilliant way of bringing together those who have goods to give and those that want to receive them. This is a real service to the donor, and house moving is a time when significant quantities of goods are discarded.

If you interrogate people asking for a collection, and then declare "it doesn't sound worth our while" you will cause outrage. At best the complainant will phone the Director of the charity, at worst she will cut the charity out of her will! Remember to be nice to potential supporters. Once you offer to collect you have to do it on request. You will certainly find yourself acting as a cheap way of getting rubbish cleared and will end up with items which will have to be taken to the municipal dump! Be courteous and good tempered. Be punctual - if people are staying in waiting for a collection they will be annoyed if they wait in for nothing. Remember in undertaking to do something on behalf of the charity you could jeopardise its good name by letting people down. It is better not to offer to do something than to offer and fail to do it. Complaints about charity shops are usually quite trivial - though strongly felt by the complainant - and one of them relates to failure to collect as promised!

As well as offering to collect, or collecting on request, charities try to collect donated goods by organising bag drops. A large, usually black plastic bag with an accompanying appeal is delivered house to house. The householder is asked to put any unwanted household items, clothing, books etc. in the bag to be collected at a specified time. The bag may be left outside the door, or the collector may stipulate a time at which he will call. Bag drops are covered by the regulations on house to house collections. These rules are currently being changed, as part of the Charities Act Part III regulations. To find out what the final rules will be contact the Institute of Charity Fund-raising Managers or the NCVO.

Bag drops may be very successful or totally hopeless. They are best organised by the shop manageress, or area organiser, using volunteers. Some charities employ casual labour to deliver and collect bags, paying on a results basis of say 10p a bag, but this is very open to fraud, as the collectors often cream off the best items for themselves, or take whole bags full to sell at car boot sales or to dealers. There is also a worry that casual labour may be less than scrupulous about distributing and collecting all the bags. The most effective bag collections are done by committed volunteers who take the opportunity to chat to people, explain the cause and what can be done with the money.

Black plastic bags can be dangerous, for example, if a child climbs into one and gets entrapped and suffocates. ROSPA has standards for black plastic film, the number of holes etc., and these should be followed by the charity. Also take care not to distribute bags to where they can be found by unsupervised, young children, who might unroll and crawl into them.

As well as appealing for second hand goods, try asking manufacturers for ends of lines. All clothing manufacturers have some samples or fag ends of ranges that they need to get rid of. If they did not they would simply be accumulating stock for they have no means of disposal, and would not have room in the factory. Large quantities will have been sold off at low prices for the winter or summer sales, but there will be single items for which there is no mechanism for selling. It is worth fostering a relationship with manufacturers, so they know that if they need to get rid of something they can just telephone and have it taken away. The reasons for manufacturers being able to do this are threefold - firstly, like everyone else, they do not like waste, secondly they do not want to incur removal costs, and you are offering a collection service and thirdly, they like to help charity - doing good, especially at no cost, is very attractive, and if you have the wit to thank them warmly, and tell them what their help means then they will give again and again.

Having to rely on donated goods means you cannot go out and buy to replace best selling items, but you can try to increase donation of certain items by 'prompting', asking for specific types of goods. For example, a sign in the window, a letter to a local newspaper, a leaflet drop asking for wedding dresses or out grown school uniform may prompt someone into action. Even though you cannot buy your stock does not mean you have to be a passive recipient. Guard against the enthusiasm of the newcomers being extinguished by the dampening gloom

> **IF YOU NEED CERTAIN TYPES OF STOCK PROMPT DONATIONS BY**
>
> - putting up a sign in the window
> - writing to the newspapers
> - leafleting
> - remind people you need what they may be willing to discard

> **MANUFACTURERS DONATING NEW GOODS** to a charity shop can claim their input VAT, but do not charge VAT on the goods donated to the charity. *Items 1 and 2, Group 16. The Zero Rate Schedule.*

of other volunteers who will always say of any initiative to drum up donated goods *"we tried that and it didn't work"* If as much energy went into doing something as explaining why it should not be done, then success would be guaranteed.

SORTING UNSALEABLE ITEMS

Not all the goods donated will be saleable. Probably half of all donated items will be discarded in the first sorting, and a further 10% may be found on close inspection to be damaged so will not be offered for sale. This does not mean they are without value, rather that they are sold to the waste merchant. There are safety restrictions which preclude the sale of some items, and some will be simply in too poor a condition to be offered for sale.

CHARITY SHOPS CANNOT SELL

- anoraks with drawstring hoods
- spectacles
- firearms (other than pre 1850)

OTHER GOODS CAN BE SOLD ONLY IF THEY CONFORM TO SAFETY STANDARDS:

- crash and cycle helmets
- riding hats
- upholstered furniture
- electrical goods
- night wear
- oil heaters
- prams, pushchairs and cots
- bunk beds
- ceramics and kitchen utensils
- gas appliances

All goods entering the shop should be examined. This should not be done on the shop floor, where it would be a safety hazard, but in the stock room or separate sorting area.

All goods should be sorted and priced before either staff or volunteers are able to buy it. Pre-selection or creaming off of the best items means the shop does not get the best stock, so is less attractive to the outside customer. The purpose of having a separate stock sorting area is not to afford those running the shop the privacy in which to go through all the stock and take the best bits for themselves, even though they pay for them, but rather to keep the shop tidy and pleasant for the customers.

The stock room layout is important. Bags should be processed systematically, one fully emptied before the next one is opened, otherwise the stock room will deteriorate into a dreadful mess. Since what lurks in the bag is unknown, it is prudent to wear rubber or cotton gloves, apron, or protective clothing and even a dust mask. One does not want to frighten the staff, so every time they plunge a hand into a plastic bag they fear a slimy encounter, but it is as well to be prudent. Sorting should take place on a table or work bench at counter level, to avoid back strain. If an individual bag is very heavy it should not be lifted onto the counter, but opened on the floor and part contents put on the work bench for sorting.

COMPLYING WITH TRADING STANDARDS LEGISLATION

Put items for disposal in a safe place - do not just heap them in a corner, making a mental note to sort them out later - because they will be potential fire or injury hazard. In particular, hard objects, hidden in a pile of clothes can lead to nasty bruising of the shins, or knocks to the head (as one bends to scoop up an apparently soft bundle and knocks ones head on a sharp corner). To prevent a stack of black plastic bags slipping down, causing accidents, or simply creating a constant need for restacking , build a 'cage' into which the bags can be stored. Ideally build rough racking, with retaining bars on the front, and a door on the bottom half, so that like a grain silo, the sacks can be tossed to the top half, and removed at the bottom.

Discard all items that are in a poor condition - for example, torn, sweat-stained, frayed, faded, cracked, chipped or foul smelling. Some discretion is needed - if an 18th century porcelain coffee-cup is cracked do not discard! This first sort is to get rid of all items not to be sold in the shop. Items that are not in very good condition will spoil the shop by repelling rather than attracting customers, who will not return as they are not hopeful of finding anything worthwhile. We all have old shabby clothes in our wardrobes, that is why we are looking for something better. Good stock will be brought down by bad stock, and this will be reflected in the prices that people will pay, just as the shop's layout and atmosphere will influence peoples perception of an appropriate price.

Immediately discard items that cannot be legally sold - anoraks with drawstring hoods, spectacles, crash and cycle helmets and riding hats, firearms (other than pre 1850 antiques), upholstered furniture (that does not conform to the 1988 Furniture and Furnishings Fire Safety regulations), night wear without fire hazard information. Some items can only be sold if they comply with safety standards that are difficult to guarantee, for example, electrical goods have to be checked and certified by a qualified electrician. It would be virtually impossible to check compliance with the safety standard of any used helmet or riding hat. Similarly, it is quite difficult to check for damage by wear and tear on prams or push chairs, so hard to ensure compliance with safety regulations. Some items may be hazardous, and it would be irresponsible to sell them, for example, old gas or oil heaters. Clearly you would not want to offer weapons, such as flick knives or even items that could be used as weapons, such as hunting knives.

Certain toys have to be labelled with clear warnings of possible risks. For example, skates and skateboards should be accompanied by the warning "Caution should be used when using this equipment, so as to avid falls or collisions causing injury. Protective equipment should be warn". (such as helmets, gloves, knee and elbow pads).

Slides or swings or similar toys have to be accompanied by instructions showing the correct assembly, and containing a warning that checks and maintenance are necessary.

If goods are packed in large plastic bags the bag should be labelled as a potential hazard, with a risk of suffocation, particularly for small children. Ceramics which are used for food and kitchen utensils must comply with safety regulations on metal release and lead levels.

Gas appliances have to comply with stringent safety standards, and would have to be checked by an expert if they are to be sold. Catalytic gas heaters must not be sold.

The local trading standards officer of the local authority should know what it is if it is permitted to sell in a charity shop. Many produce useful booklets. Legislation and regulations change, and it is prudent to conduct a six monthly check with the trading standards officer to see if there have been any changes or if any are likely. The Consumer Safety Unit of the Department of Trade and Industry should be able to supply information.

The European Community issues directives intermittently which have a bearing on what may or may not be sold in charity shops. The local trading standards office is expected to keep abreast of them! It was thought that EC regulations on toy safety would preclude the sale of second hand toys but in fact the rule allows the sale of toys, if properly labelled, and conforming to safety standards.

Apart from goods that must not be sold by law, there is a duty to conform to the Sale of Goods Act, 1979, which stipulates that goods should be of merchantable quality, and the General Product Safety Directive of the European Community.

The charity has its good name to protect, and that means that it would want to adopt a higher standard than simply conforming with the law. Think about what you are offering for sale. Could it be harmful? Do not assume people follow instructions, or use items for the purpose intended. Of course, virtually anything can be dangerous if misused - tights could be used as a noose or one could choke on clothes if one ate them. Be sensible. Consider if you would feel happy with the item in a home with small children. Do not assume people are as careful or thoughtful as you. Weigh the few pounds or pence an item might raise against the damage to the charity's reputation if someone was injured or killed by a product sold by one of its shops.

SORTING CLOTHES

Failure to be sufficiently ruthless in discarding sub-standard stock is a very usual fault in charity shops, and one that headquarter and area managers struggle hard to rectify. Typically volunteers, who cannot bear waste, and are old enough to have lived through the privation of wartime, will think they are doing their best for the charity by cramming into the shop all available stock - but 'make do and mend' is not in the minds of modern day shoppers. They come to a charity shop in the same way they would go to any other shop, except they expect a larger variety of clothes, more frequently changing stock and access to clothes originally more expensive

> **BE RUTHLESS IN DISCARDING STOCK**
>
> Good stock is brought down by bad stock.
>
> People pay less in shops where the stock is shabby, even though the item they are buying is in perfect condition.

and of better quality than they could afford. Except for teenagers and art college students no one wants to be identified as dressing at a charity shop, so the clothes must not be distinctive because they are worn or shabby.

Discarded items should be sold for scrap, to rag merchants and scrap merchants. Pre-sort in the correct categories to get the best prices, and store safely for collection. If you have enough volunteers you can encourage them to salvage anything saleable from the discarded items, for example, to remove buttons and bag them up in little cellophane bags for sale, or cut up cotton prints

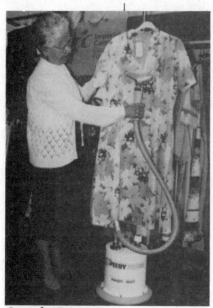

Speedy Press

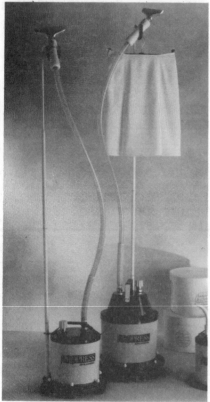

Propress

into squares for patchwork. There are quite a lot of uses for discarded clothes - for example really enthusiastic volunteers could make rag rugs or patchwork quilts or dolls clothes, but the price they could charge in the context of the charity shop maybe discouragingly low. If the standard of the work is wonderful it is better to raffle the larger items, such as patchwork quilts and use it as a focal point in the shop window. Do not forget to send the story to the local newspaper or radio station.

Items which are judged to be saleable should be hung on a rail for pricing sizing and pressing. Very few shops will go to the expense of dry cleaning or laundering donated items (though the public often assumes everything is cleaned). Since generally up to a third of the goods donated and put on display will not actually sell, but will end up with the rag merchant, it is rarely cost effective to pay for cleaning. In some cases, with garments which could command a high price, for example model coats or suits, it may be worth the risk. A good compromise is to use a portable steamer, a machine that looks like an industrial vacuum cleaner, and with which one can get the creases out of a hanging garment, and give a really fresh, well pressed look. Manufacturers include Propress in London and Speedy in North Shields, (see Resources section.) For most charity shops the smaller models giving about an hour's continuous use would be sufficient. Those using the steamer must be warned to take care, as they can burn themselves if they are careless.

All garments should be sized. Either this information can be taken from the label, or everything can be measured and sized from a chart, which should be hung on the wall of the stock room. Perhaps take a lesson from a well known multinational fashion house and label all women's clothes, other than shoes, a size smaller - so a size 12 will fit someone who normally takes a size 14. The potential for chaos is enormous, but since most women would be cheered up if they could get into a smaller size it may make for more satisfied customers! When you size garments use colour coded sizing cubes, which slip over the handle of the hanger, as this will make it easier to identify, and enable you to see at a glance what sizes need replenishing on the rails.

Hanger, Tie Hooks & Display Clips

All garments should be hung on proper hangers, not disposable wire ones but proper wooden or good quality plastic ones. Different types of garments need different hangers - men's suits and jackets look better, and therefore command higher prices, if they are displayed on a shaped hanger. Trousers and skirts need to be on special hangers, otherwise they will be forever slipping off and need picking up and pressing. It may seem extravagant to go out and buy hangers, and very tempting to get them donated from local clothes shops or dry cleaners, or collect spares from home, but the stock is so varied it helps the overall appearance of the shop if the clothes can be hung at the same heights, with some coherence. Having odd hangers just adds to the jumble effect, and detracts from the perceived value. To help those sorting the stock display a sign in the stock room showing which hanger to use for which item, and showing where to position the label.

All garments should be labelled, with the size, the price, and the date it was first put on display. The label should also carry a message about the work of the Charity - along the lines of "Black Bottom Charity, a registered charity, providing care for retired chorus girls. Thank you for your support." The amount of charity message is really a matter of taste, but generally the simpler and more positive the message, the better.

STOCK LOOKS BETTER AND SELLS FOR MORE IF IT IS

- hung on a proper hanger
- labelled with standard labels
- steam pressed
- not crammed in to the rail

As well as price, size and kill by date each item may be marked with a stock number. Those with chains of shops, for example, Oxfam or the British Red Cross, provide their shops with printed labels. The Oxfam label has the price printed on tickets which are supplied for an enormous range of prices, from pence up to tens of pounds. The central charity shops' unit will, from experience, know for which prices to produce the most tickets. The Oxfam tickets also carry the disclaimers that the size is approximate "for guidance only" and that " unless otherwise shown this item is made up from mixed or miscellaneous fibres", both statements show awareness of consumer protection legislation!

The date on which the item was put on display is best shown by a code number. Alternatively you can mark 'the kill by' date, the date at which the item would be taken off display. Simple codes, such as 195 for week 1 1995, or 1195 for 1st January, 1995 can be used. Most people find it easier to work out sequences of numbers rather than letters of the alphabet.

• OXFAM •

£2.29

**APPROXIMATE SIZE
FOR GUIDANCE ONLY**

CODE

UNLESS OTHERWISE SHOWN THIS ITEM IS MADE UP
FROM MIXED OR MISCELLANEOUS FIBRES

*Thankyou
for shopping with us*

• OXFAM •

Garments can be numbered and listed in a stock book as they are put on sale. The number is simply crossed out in the book when the item is sold (the label is removed when the customer pays, and the labels collected at the end of the day). This is a method of stock control, a check that the money in the till tallies with the sales and stock records. Not all charity shops bother to record stock. They take the view that since the stock is donated, there is no need to account for it to the auditors. If through put is considerable, the task of listing might be onerous. To use the numbering system as a check on stock losses would mean that periodic stock takes would be needed, which would not only require a great deal of effort, but also disrupt trade (since it is nigh impossible to stock take when the shop is open). On balance, most charity shop organisers dispense with a stock taking system. Certainly if staff were being paid it would probably not be cost effective since the cost of recording and monitoring would be greater than the value of the stock which might go astray.

A full-scale stock-control system might not be necessary or desirable but a numbering system can be used to provide a great deal of useful information, as a basis for management action, by monitoring what sells. How you gather the information varies. A stock numbering system can indicate the category of clothing, and other details such as its size and price. The information can be taken off the label, or from a stock book. It can be keyed in to the till, through the dissection buttons, when ringing up the sale. A simple list kept by the cash desk noting sales of the day can give the hard information on what sizes, and types of garment are selling. This is much more reliable than anecdotal evidence. It is usual for people to believe that what they like sells, and that what they dislike does not. Keeping records provides more reliable information. Collecting information is not the end purpose, which is to use the information as a basis for action. For example, if you find you are selling men's overcoats at the rate of one a day, at least when you have them, you can make an appeal for men's overcoats. If you find size 10 clothes never sell you might be more rigorous in your sorting, and offer relatively few for sale. You should offer as big a selection as possible of the items and

> Offer as big a selection as you can of items and sizes that sell. Give space to each type of goods in proportion to its popularity

sizes that sell. The space you give to each category should be in proportion to its popularity. For example, if you sell more women's separates than anything else, display more of them than anything else.

Garments should be dated, so they can be 'killed off' once they have been on display and failed to sell, say after four weeks. The 'killing off' system has to be used if the shop is not to be swamped with unsold, and unsaleable, stock and to retain customer interest. Charity shops have very committed regular customers, who will visit the shop several times a week, in the hope of spotting a bargain. In conventional shops the stock changes relatively infrequently, so the customer does not have to keep returning just to see what is there. In the best charity shop the stock changes daily.

Your space is limited, and you have to make it work for you, by having stock that sells. You cannot afford to display goods that do not sell, so after the item has had its chance it has to be removed and replaced by newly received stock. It is heart-breaking to discard good quality garments, but you have to be ruthless, to retain customer interest. If it has not sold in four weeks it probably will not sell in four months. The 'kill off' date may be two weeks after being put out on display, or it may be six weeks. This will depend on the availability of your space, and the amount of donated stock you are managing to attract. Being able to change the stock often will retain customers interest, and is an

> **STOCK** should be given a period in which to sell - say 2 to 6 weeks - then ruthlessly discarded.
>
> **'KILL BY'** discard rates vary, depending on availability of stock and space:
>
> - Age Concern   3 weeks
> - Tenovus   1 week
> - National Children's Home   3 weeks
> - Salvation Army   3 weeks
> - Animal Welfare Trust   4 weeks

important factor in improving sales. To some extent the time scale is determined by the availability of other replacement stock.

Stock that has failed to sell by its 'kill by' date, can be offered at half price on a bargain rail. Some shops prefer not to do this because space is limited, and they believe it undercuts the fully priced items. It is something worth experimenting with. A bargain rail does not have to be a permanent feature of the shop, it can be used from time to time to stimulate trade.

AIM TO SELL 80% OF THE GOODS YOU DISPLAY

If you are selling less consider:

- are your prices too high

- are the goods the wrong things in the wrong sizes

- should you be more ruthless in sorting

The charity that manages to sell 80% of what it displays is doing well. If you are not achieving rates any where near to that level review your pricing, is it too high compared to the competition? Is the quality of the goods you are offering poor? Are they the wrong sorts of goods for your customers? It is no good offering ball gowns if your customers want warm work clothes. If you are selling at least 80% of certain types of goods, but much less in other categories, try to increase the quantity of goods in the popular category by soliciting donated goods of that type.

If you keep a stock room from which you can bring stock forward as needed, it is important to start the dating from the time the garment is put on display not when it is received and labelled. Aim to get your goods sorted and labelled and on display on the same day as you receive it.

It is best to attach tickets on the waist band of trousers or skirts and the sleeve of all jackets, sweaters, dresses. Sleeveless dresses can be labelled at the back neck. Labels can be attached using a tagging gun, which 'shoots' a plastic thread through the garment. It has to be cut off, so is safer than a pinned or tied label.

Decide whether you are going to store unseasonal items (such as winter coats received in summer, or cotton dresses received in January). Sometimes lack of storage space will force you to put the item on sale. Some charity shops have the space to set stock aside, and bring it forward at the time when customer interest is highest. Those with chains of shops sometimes warehouse centrally, or even sort and price centrally. There are arguments in favour of central warehousing - namely, the ability to store and distribute stock in the quantity and category needed. The disadvantage that individual shop managers feel aggrieved that they are not allowed to exercise control, but are being given what others judge appropriate (although this can be overcome by allowing the manager to select from the warehouse). Running a warehouse and collecting and delivering goods involves extra costs, and a charity has to look carefully at the figures to see if having a warehouse is cost effective. Those shops which are most successful at attracting donated goods often feel aggrieved if they are not allowed their pick, before the surplus items are sent away to other shops.

If a shop attracts enormous quantities of donated goods, or if as a result of a particular appeal or special collection, the charity finds itself with bags of goods, it will need to work out a method of sorting and distributing to other shops. The simplest is to take the unsorted bags to whichever shop needs the most stock, and for them to treat it as they would any donated stock. It might be best to have the goods sorted at the shop with the best sorting facilities, and the space in which to store the bags during the sorting. The really important thing is to anticipate the influx of goods. Bad decisions are more likely when everyone is irritable because they are tripping over bags of old clothes.

> **AN EXPERIENCED SORTER** can deal with 40-45 garments an hour.

PRICING GARMENTS

More money is lost to the charity through the underpricing of goods than for any other reason. What you can charge will depend on the location of the shop and the clientele it attracts. A shop in Sloane Square, Chelsea reports no price resistance to selling tweed jackets at £25 and ladies suits at between £40 and £60. Clearly these prices are a fraction of the original price, probably an average of 20%, but it would be unrealistic to expect to sell the same items for even half the amount in most other areas. The customer will measure the value of the goods not just in relation to its original price, but also against what a new skirt or coat might cost from the shops she might use. A Christian Dior original might have cost thousands of pounds but that does not make it worth £500 to the customer buying it in a charity shop. So the generally held formula which says charge 20% of the original price for goods that are in perfect

> **UNDER PRICING** of donated stock is the biggest loss to the charity. Aim to charge 20% of the original price if the goods are in near perfect condition.

condition can only be applied up to a certain level, above which it is hard to go. It would be unusual for the cost of any one item, except for wedding dresses, to be above £50, and that figure would be too high for many areas.

Why do those working in charity shops generally under-price goods - in the opinion of area-managers and head-quarters staff? Do they in fact, as they argue, know their area and customers better? It is true that you will sell more items at lower prices - but will you sell twice as much if prices are halved? Probably not, since the range that can be offered is restricted to what you are given, and the customer knowing that a speedy decision is needed, since there is only one of a kind, and it might be snapped up, is less price sensitive than in a conventional shop, since the garment will generally still be much less than elsewhere.

Shop managers and supervisors are keen to please their customers. They want to be popular with them, and that inclines them to lower rather than raise prices. They know that for some of the customers, money is very tight, and they naturally want to help. The problem for the charity is that its beneficiaries are not generally its customers, but rather causes such as cancer research or the provision of a hospice. The charity owes a duty to get the most money it can for its charitable purpose.

Undercharging can also upset the donors of the goods, who must, if their goodwill is to be retained, feel that their contribution was worthwhile, and fairly priced. "Fairness" is very important in pricing goods. The customer should feel that the relative costs make sense - so if a wool skirt is £4 , a wool skirt with a designer label could be £5 and a size 8 mini-skirt could be £2.

It is sensible to have guide-line prices for different types of garments. A basic price for say a dress could be increased or decreased depending on condition, style and colour, and manufacturer. High fashion items, in medium or large sizes, may command a premium. You can vary prices, and experiment with them. See at which point there is price resistance. Compare what other charity shops are charging for comparable items.

The psychology of pricing is a fine art in retailing. Never have a price that is unusual - like 67p or £3.21 - because it strikes people as odd and makes them stop and think about the price, whereas you want them to be thinking about the product, and how nice it would be to have it. Try to offer goods over a range of prices, so the customer can exercise choice, but also try to make the reasons for price differentials obvious otherwise the customer will be uneasy. Watch the customer to see if they lose interest once they see the price tag. Talk to them. John Tough, a leading authority on charity shops, argues that "unless you get two to three complaints a week about your pricing you are probably under-pricing."

Charities with large chains of shops usually try to give guide-lines on pricing. Most typically they suggest a formula which is a base price for the category of item (say £2 for a shirt). Then a list of criteria are given which enhance the value. So if the shirt is unworn the price can be enhanced by 100%. If it is by a well known maker of it can be enhanced 25% - 100%, depending on the make. Marks and Spencer may enhance 25%, Pierre Cardin 100%. Similarly, if the item is in fair but not excellent condition it may be discounted 25%. By giving an actual scale it is hoped that some measure of consistency is achieved, particularly where there is more than one person pricing garments. Above all that the pricing should seem fair to the customer.

HAVE GUIDE-LINES FOR PRICES
Give a base price for the item
Increase the price:
• if the garment is new
• If it is by a well known designer
• If it is in a popular size
reduce from the base line:
• if it is not in excellent condition
• if it is in a difficult colour or material

See what department stores such as Marks and Spencer or British Home Stores charge for certain base items - like wool jumpers, white shirts, summer dresses, men's jackets. Note the prices each year, and consider whether your prices are keeping in line with inflation. If you are selling nearly everything you put on sale, you can probably afford to put your prices up. If you are failing to sell most of your stock, then over-pricing may be a factor.

SORTING BRIC A BRAC, BOOKS, STAMPS ETC.

As well as clothes charity shops receive donations of unwanted household goods, books, toys and bric a brac. Some are new, some are the dregs from the spring cleaning of old cupboards. Because the range is so huge it is very difficult to value them correctly, particularly as people collect and pay a premium for such strange things - like old teddy bears and old scientific instruments. Unless you have amongst your volunteers a real expert with an enormous eclectic knowledge it is very difficult to get the correct pricing of bric a brac. There is also the problem that people pay prices appropriate to the surroundings in which they are buying - for example, a 19th century Staffordshire figure may be £250 in an antique shop in Kensington, but would sit for a long time in a charity shop in Worksop at even half the price. Most charity shop organisers recognise this and after taking expert advice send more expensive items for sale at auction (but remember auction prices are considerably lower than antique shop prices).

Volunteers should be encouraged to be realistic about the price bric a brac can raise in the context of the charity shop. There is an enormous difference between the buying and selling price in the antiques business. Dealers with shops generally only pay half of their selling price for their stock. Millers Price Guides may be useful in getting some idea of prevailing prices, but generally the prices quoted are higher than you will be able to command because of the context. New items in their original wrapping will also have to be discounted if they are to sell - possibly by as much as 50%, though it depends on the desirability of the item.

When bric a brac is brought into the shop it will have to be sorted. The first thing is to discard all the items that cannot be sold by law - for example, cycling helmets or uncertified electrical goods. Then some items will be weeded out as unsuitable, such as pornographic material. Out, too, will go goods that could be dangerous if improperly used - for example, hunting knives and things in poor condition, such as chipped enamel saucepans or jigsaws with pieces missing. Just as clothes have to be rejected if not of good merchantable quality, so too with bric a brac. The problem is that with antique items, collected for their historical significance, rather than their usefulness, it is not always easy to tell if it should be discarded. When sorting clothing the rule is "when in doubt chuck it out". With bric a brac the reverse prevails "when in doubt, ask". Who you ask depends on where you are and what it is. For most items a local antiques dealer or jeweller or auctioneer will be sufficiently knowledgeable. If you suspect you have something that might be really valuable it might be worth taking it in or sending a photograph of it to a top auction house. The local museum often offers a free consultation and identification service (not valuations) which could be helpful. If one of your volunteers is a retired jeweller or antique dealer, on whose expertise you rely, take care that they keep abreast of fluctuations in the market prices. With donations of jewellery, except for very obviously cheap, intrinsically valueless pieces like plastic beads, valuations are important. If selling hallmarked silver and gold you are required to display a hallmark chart (obtainable from the British Hallmarking Council, Birmingham). Remember when pricing jewellery, the attractiveness of the item is still the key to its price - unless you are given a ring with a very valuable gemstone in a horrible setting. It is the workmanship and design which really count, and pieces of jewellery of intrinsic value, because of the material it is made from should almost certainly be sold to a dealer.

Some sorted items can be priced and put straight into stock, since there is not much doubt as to its value. For example, Cornish Ware blue and white striped china or Brown Betty tea pots do not need to be independently valued. Anything on which an opinion is needed should be listed, before being removed, and checked in and out of the valuations stock book.

With books look out for first editions and signed copies. Remember people collect bindings, so although the text might be terrible the cover may command a premium. Build up a relationship with an antiquarian book shop, and ask their advice. Try to attract as a volunteer a keen bibliophile, who could keep a weather-eye on the donated books, and perhaps sell the more valuable items to a specialist dealer. If you group books by subject, for example, gardening or needlework or cookery, then you will enhance their value, increase sales and build up a regular clientele.

Bric a brac should be priced either using a stick on label, from a pricing gun, or with a tie-on jewellery ticket. It helps to increase its value if it can be 'provenanced', that is some information is given about its age, use and origin. For example, *"Cereal dish. Blue transfer on cream ware. Late 19th century Staffordshire ware."* Be careful to add a disclaimer - *"information is given in good faith but should be verified by the purchaser"* - so that an irate customer does not sue under the Trades Description Act, if an attribution proves wrong.

Bric a brac can add interest to the charity shop window, and in the shop, but it is quite difficult to display well since many of the items are small. Too often the display of bric a brac is dribbled along a shelf, cheap pressed glass next to a Crown Derby cup and saucer, next to a Spong hand mincer. This detracts from the value and desirability of all the items. Kitchen items like rolling pins should be piled, perhaps into an old shopping basket. More valuable, delicate items, the sort that would be displayed in a china cabinet in the drawing room, should be put in a glazed, well-lit display cabinet, which will raise its perceived value, and justify its relatively high price.

It is very important that whoever is responsible for the sorting of books or bric a brac does not cream off the best items. They must be independently valued if necessary, and always priced before anyone can buy them. The pricing should not be done by the purchaser. If a volunteer who normally prices, say antique jewellery, wants to buy a particular item, and it is quite in order that they should want to do so, it is essential to get a second independent valuation, because failure to do so could lead to accusations of impropriety. This rule should be made quite clear at the time the staff, voluntary or paid, start working in the shop, and not produced like a white rabbit out of the hat at the time when the situation arises, since this will lead to ill feeling all round.

By virtue of being on site, the shop staff are inevitably in a privileged position in getting the pick of the stock. But the charity has to ensure that a fair price is paid, irrespective of the buyer, and that the scale of 'creaming off' is not so substantial that the customers do not get any chance of the good stock. It is also a question of scale. Whilst it is acceptable for a volunteer to buy goods for themselves and their families it is not acceptable for them to re-sell items, even though they have paid for them, because it is breach of trust. Again this should be made quite clear from the outset.

Those working in the shop must owe their first duty to the shop and its well-being, and not have a vested interest in keeping prices low or discarding stock. Similarly, if you are selling items to a dealer (a jeweller or antique shop owner) take care not to form too close a relationship lest you are accused of favouring one company, with the implication that you are not doing your best for the charity. Do not be gullible. Because someone says *"I always do my best for you, because I want to support your charity"* that is not a reason to believe them. You must be more prudent in protecting the charity's interests than you would be in protecting your own, since you are in a position of trust, and when sorting and pricing donated stock is a good time to remember it!

DISPOSING OF UNSOLD STOCK

A major part of running a charity shop is finding a way of disposing profitably of the donated goods that cannot or do not sell in the shop. Since this may be as much as 80% of the goods donated, setting up a disposal system from the start is essential.

Virtually all textiles can be recycled, it is only an estimated 5% of all textile waste that cannot be salvaged because of excessive soiling, and that is not likely to be amongst the clothing brought into a charity shop. The rag merchants (now stylishly renamed textile reclamation companies) want to buy textiles, which they can sort and process in a variety of ways. An estimated 15-20% are sold as clothing to Third World countries (thus undermining the indigenous clothing industry, so be specific if you do not want your charity's surpluses going for such purposes). 40% will be turned into wiping cloths for industrial use. 20% will be used as filling material for installation and around 15% will be re-spun. The Reclamation Association gives a splendid example of successful re-cycling -

> *"a pullover is kept by a purchaser for 7 years before being discarded, after grading and processing this would probably re-appear as over-coating material with a life span of a further 7 years: it could then re-appear as a blanket again with a use of probably 7 years before finally ending up in either filling materials for a mattress or as roofing felt."*

Since it is estimated that 4% of the household waste is textiles, amounting to 3/4 million tons nation-wide which have to be disposed of by local authority refuse collectors at a cost of £20 a household, it is clearly desirable for charities to persuade more households to bring their old clothes into a charity shop. Even if the clothes cannot be sold as garments, they can be sold to waste merchants.

The Reclamation Association, which is based in Huntingdon, will provide a list of members who are prepared to buy from charity shops, and offer a regular collection service. The prices offered by the different companies vary, and it is difficult to compare prices as some quote a figure per tonne, some per kilo and some per bag. Some collect unsorted waste at a flat rate, others offer a range of prices depending on the type of material. Some have a very low minimum collection (20 bags), others want at least a tonne a time. It is worth ringing around, and seeing what is on offer, and what suits your requirements best.

Review the position at least annually to see if you are happy with the service. Could it be bettered? Is someone else offering a higher rate? Do not judge only on the price paid, as that is only one factor, consider also whether you are getting a friendly helpful service. Is the collection dependable? Do they leave a trail of litter from broken bags, or do they clear up any spillage? The quality of service is particularly important if you are working with a large number of volunteers. If the waste merchants are unpleasant they will make your volunteers not want to come and help.

Work with your waste merchant. Ask if there are ways of increasing your income from the waste. Would you get more if you pre-sort, and if so into what categories? What does he pay top rates for? Is there a particular shortage that you could respond to? Try to optimise your income from waste. There are about 50 different UK companies who recycle textiles, and it is worthwhile making sure that you are getting the best deal possible.

5
SECURITY

Break-ins

Shoplifting

Theft by staff

Rules for cash handling

SECURITY

Charity shops are not exempt from theft because the profits are used for a good cause. This may make the theft more morally reprehensible, but it does not safeguard the property. Because the majority of the stock is donated, there is rarely the same degree of stock control that conventional retailers use, so it is difficult to gauge the likely level of stock loss. Generally, it is judged by those charities with a chain of shops, to be around 10%.

BREAK-INS

Losses arise in a variety of ways. Relatively unimportant, though it may happen repeatedly to one particular shop, or in one particular area, are the break-ins. These happen when the shops are closed. The method of entry may be through a roof light, a window or a smashed in door. If one were going to break into a shop, a charity shop would probably not seem to hold out the most chance of loot! However, to the burglar looking for a relatively modest amount of cash, it may still be an attractive choice. The damage and subsequent vandalism caused in the break-in is likely to be more costly than the cash or goods stolen.

Think about the security of the premises when looking for a shop site. The best precaution is to bar all rear windows, so even if forced open, no-one can crawl through (it also stops bags full of goods being passed out).

> ### MOST BREAK-INS ARE OPPORTUNISTIC
>
> Make it hard for the casual thief to break-in.
>
> - bar back windows
> - deadlock doors
> - empty the till - and leave the empty cash drawer open
> - do not keep cash on the premises overnight
> - light entrances

Never leave money, except a modest float well hidden, on the premises over-night. Bank the takings every day. Leave the till drawer open so the fact it is empty can be seen. Make sure skylights are locked. Do not leave the key in the front door, or the backdoor unlocked. It might be worth installing a burglar alarm, or a time switch on the shop lights, so the shop interior is visible to passers-by up until midnight. Both these can be deterrents, but only if the shop is in an area where there are passers-by. Similarly, a light with a sensor which switches itself on when people approach may deter a thief. Most 'break ins' are opportunistic, so by making it relatively difficult, the casual thief will be deterred.

There is very little to be done to protect against the vandal who decides to chuck a brick through your window, to attract attention, or because they are hallucinating. In that case your task is to reassure your staff that it is unlikely to happen again, and keep everyone calm.

As well as securing your premises, just as you would as a sensible householder, you should also make sure you are insured. You cannot insure against all types of theft, except at unrealistically high premiums, but you can insure the premises against damage from break-ins, including the shop fittings, and against stock and cash losses. There will usually be an 'excess', which means you have to pay the first tranche of the damage, but you can at least claim. Losses from shop lifting are very difficult to claim for on any insurance policy. The 'excess' may mean you never reach the level for which a claim can be made. The mere fact that something is missing is not likely to make much of a case to the insurer, who will want precise details as to who stole it and when.

Do make sure all the staff are aware that there is an insurance policy, what cover is offered, and the procedure for making a claim - or reporting an incident to the area manager or head office so a claim could be made. Keep the information on record in the shop information file in a drawer by the till.

SHOP-LIFTING

Break-ins are unusual. Shop-lifting is a daily problem. The shop-lifter may steal the odd garment, or may be more ambitious and take a quantity of garments at a time. If the shop is in an orderly condition rather than a massive jumble sale it will be easier to spot losses, to see what is missing on the rail, or indeed if the whole rail has gone missing! Rails should not be crammed with stock. How many garments will fit on a metre rail varies - fewer winter coats than silk blouses! As a rule of thumb, you should be able to push the stock into two-thirds of the rail, leaving the other third empty. That gives enough space for customers to flick through the rail. (And remember if you do not cram the rails full the air circulating around the garments will help to keep the shop sweet-smelling.)

Thinking how the merchandise leaves the shop will alert you to the possibilities of preventing the theft. It is a truism to say that goods are carried out by the shop-lifter. How do they conceal them - in shopping bags, under their clothing, hidden at the bottom of push chairs. Be suspicious of customers carrying large bags. Offer to look after them so the customer can free both hands to look round the shop. (Merely knowing that they have been noticed is the biggest deterrent to the shop lifter). Be suspicious of customers wearing large, voluminous coats, particularly if the weather is clement.

THE BIGGEST DETERRENT TO SHOPLIFTERS is knowing they have been observed, and that staff are watchful. Greet all customers. Remind them of your presence and vigilance.

Watch customers. Are people behaving atypically? For example most customers look at one or two rails of clothes in their own sizes, or for other members of the family. Often the shop-lifter acts in an unusual way, paying more attention to the shop staff and their movements rather than the stock. Typically, they move from one section to the other without looking properly at the stock. They may be ill at ease. Watch customers hands, not just their faces. After all, they steal with their hands.

Beware of the customers who appear to be making a huge fuss, they may be creating a diversion so that their partners can stuff goods into a basket unobserved. Professional gangs of shop-lifters can send someone ahead to remove stock from the rails, and hide it in a prearranged place. They often work in teams and the first team will include someone to act as a decoy, by involving the staff in complicated enquiries. The follow up team then collects the clothing, unobserved, and leaves the shop. Staff are often suspicious of these teams, and will say afterwards *"We thought they were up to something but did not know what to do"*. The shop-lifters deliberately confuse the staff, and try to fluster them. The best defence is to be obviously alert.

Get the message across to any potential shop lifters that you have noticed their presence, and will remember them. Greet all customers. Remind them of your continued presence by offering to help, or make conversation about the weather. Tidy up goods near to them. Staff should, in effect, patrol the shop, circulating so that every part of the shop and every customer is kept under observation. If you feel you are being deliberately distracted, say very clearly that you are sorry you cannot help them just now, but will deal with their enquiry later, if they could come back. Stand firmly behind the till which should be your best vantage point. You may loose genuine customers, but generally if your suspicions are aroused there is good reason. Go with your instinct.

The fitting room, if you have one, may provide the seclusion the shop-lifter needs. It may help to have curtains not down to the ground, but say 18 inches from the floor so you can watch, for example if bags are being filled. Post a member of staff outside the changing room to check the number of garments taken in to be tried on, and that the same number are returned. Be aware that people switch price tags. The plastic thread punched through to secure the label gives some protection against this, as the tag needs cutting off - but people have been known to carry a pricing gun and switch labels from a low priced to a high priced garment. The best protection is for the staff to know the stock, and its correct price.

Be careful not to make things easier for the thief. Do not have mirrors they can tuck price tickets or even garments behind. Keep the changing room clear of unwanted stock, so that it is easy to tell what is going in and coming out. Be careful about letting customers take shopping bags into changing rooms. Offer to look after them behind the counter. Push chairs or shopping trolleys should not be taken into the changing room.

What do you do if you see someone removing stock and secreting it away? Because of the problems of accusing people unjustly, particularly if they have not left the premises with the goods, it is probably best to simply ask them *"Would you like to pay for the goods in your bag?"* or *"Shall I take the money for those things?"* Most people, when challenged will make an excuse along the lines of *"Oh yes, I forgot"* and pay for the goods. You can ask them not to come back. You do not have to give a reason, just say you do not want them to come back.

If someone leaves the premises with goods you can make a citizen's arrest, and phone the police. Whilst one would not want to condone crime, it has to be said that for most charity shop staff it would be better to challenge the shop-lifter and invite them to pay for the goods, rather than trying to apprehend them. Once the police are involved, then it is up to them to decide whether to prosecute or give a caution, or not to proceed. The shop staff will be called upon as witnesses to give evidence. All staff should be told not to challenge a shop-lifter who might be violent. Simply call the police as soon as possible.

If someone demands cash from the till; better to give the money than risk injury. However often one gives this advice there is always someone so outraged that without thinking they will try to fight off the would be robber. Try to drill it into all staff, voluntary or paid, that if menaced just hand over the money, because if they resist, they put not just themselves but their colleagues at risk. It is better all round if no violence is used, and resisting may panic the already nervous burglar into action. Calm during any attack is the golden rule.

Thefts from the till are less frequent than theft of stock. Most arises through carelessness, when the till is left unattended, with the keys in, or when cash is counted and bagged, ready for banking, and one of the bags left by the side of the till, and picked up by an opportunistic thief. Collecting boxes left by the till should be secured, and emptied regularly so in the event of theft the damage is minimised. Sometimes, if the till drawer is left open an agile thief may reach over and pull out the notes. Common sense over cash handling will provide the best protection.

Do not keep large amounts of money in the till. Bank daily, if not several times a day. If money has to be kept on the premises overnight keep it in a safe. Do not hang the safe keys up next to it! Keep large notes at the back of the till drawer. Screw the till down, or weight it so that it cannot be snatched up easily. Do not count money in the sales area. Work out a strategy for paying into the bank. Have a night safe facility. Vary the times at which money is banked. If you are fearful of the safety of your staff on the way to the bank arrange cash to be collected by a security firm. You will have to negotiate a special rate but the cost may be around £5 a collection. It may be worth it to you.

Be aware of professional forgers who seem particularly fond of charity shops as targets for getting their notes into circulation. Charity shops have mainly cash transactions and also are staffed by those who are seen as less experienced, or frankly doddery, which is their attraction for forgers. A

> Be wary of the customer who pays for a relatively small purchase with a high denomination note. It may be a forgery. Similarly, avoid giving change for high denomination notes.

purchase is made, and paid for with a large denomination note. Change is given. The note is forged, and the charity is the loser. Make all staff aware of the problem. You may wish to refuse to change any £50 notes - simply say you have not got the change. Ask the police to alert you as to the forgeries prevailing at any one time.

Another trick to get money from the till is for a "customer" to ask for change. [They may make a small purchase.] They produce a note and when counting out the change you will be interrupted by their accomplice, or they may simply by their aggressive manner with constant talk, completely confuse you. They then claim you have short-changed them, or they retain the note for which you are giving change, but claim to have given it to you. Their aim is to confuse, fluster and bully. Being aware that you may be being set up is half the battle. As a general rule, do not give change. If you feel you are being railroaded, take a deep breath and stop. Then refuse to give change, explain you cannot open the till except for a sale. Blame headquarters, commiserate with the 'customer' and say you would of course like to help, but do not open the till. If you are being flustered when giving change, close the till. Explain you cannot give change if you are being flustered. Call help - they can act as a witness. If the punter claims you have short-changed them, and you are sure you have not, and you are fairly sure it is a trick then bring a procedure form asking them to fill in their details, and write in to head office for their refund. There is no way of dealing with these attempts to defraud without a residual nasty taste in the mouth. If you are duped you will feel terrible, and angry. And if you are not, you can never be certain that you were right in believing that you have thwarted a fraudster. Do not brood on it too much, or let your volunteers brood on it, as it will adversely affect staff morale.

THEFT BY STAFF

More worrying than stock leaving through the front door is stock leaving through the backdoor, because it is likely to be in more substantial quantities. Generally, stock losses through the back door are done with the collusion of a member of the shop's staff. Though it has been known for outsiders to bring a van to the back entrance, walk in through an unlocked back door, and load up quantities of donated goods, it is not usual (after all, stealing from an electrical suppliers, for example, would generate more profit for the same risk). More usual is an insider, one of the staff, arranging to leave the door open, or even passing bags of goods out to the waiting thief. Sometimes a whole shift in the shop may be in league. They might have deliberately planned to ingratiate themselves as volunteers, offer to do the sorting *"I prefer to work behind the scenes"* and set up a supply system for a relatives second-hand clothes business. In other cases people may be corrupted by another member of staff, or finding themselves unwittingly involved not want to "sneak."

It should be made absolutely clear to all staff, at the time of recruitment, and emphasised during their induction, that connection with any business involving second hand clothes or bric a brac must be declared, and no item donated to the shop may be re-sold by any member of staff, their family or friends. Nor should they enable others to do so. Such action would be regarded as a dismissable offence.

Keep a rough count of items in and whether it is packed for the rag merchant or put out on display. This can be done on a rough count basis of bags or items. If by bags it is possible to get a rough idea of numbers of garments in a bag by carrying out random sampling. This is not designed to be an accurate stock take. It is simply to give an idea of the relative scale of things, as a basis for action. For example, are more donated goods brought in on a Tuesday or on a Friday? If so you can plan extra staff for sorting. Is it suspicious? Can you account for these variations? Do they happen only when certain staff are in the shop? If they are on holiday is the pattern broken? Are they "creaming" off stock? Do the number of sacks for the waste merchant vary from day to day? Is it because some of the sorters are much slower than others? (Speedy sorters can deal with around 40-45 garments an hour). Having information keeps you on top of the situation. It will help you use resources most effectively, and will alert you to possible problems, including theft.

The best defence against this "insider dealing" is the vigilance of the shop staff, and in particular the shop manager (though it may be the shop manager who is perpetrating the theft). The biggest deterrent to crime is the fear of being caught.

There are simple, practical safeguards to preventing stock leaving through the back door. Firstly, and most obviously, keep the door shut against opportunistic intruders. Put a bell over the door, or under a mat-well by the door, which rings whenever the door

> The biggest deterrent to theft is the fear of being caught. Create systems which expose shortfalls quickly.

is opened. It may be that an old fashioned shop bell, on a spring, would be better than an electrical system which can be immobilised. [An old coil bell can be immobilised, but much less easily and inconspicuously.] Train the staff, both paid and volunteer, to be alert to the ringing of the back door bell. Is it more frequent than usual? Go and see why.

Never leave staff in the sorting room by themselves for any length of time. Pop in unexpectedly throughout the day. Soft heeled shoes will not announce your impending arrival. If you have any suspicion of an individual or a team, watch carefully, and switch the rota so they are working with people you can trust. Raise the worry, without accusation, with all the staff saying you fear that there are stock losses. This should alert everyone, and encourage the maleficent to move on. This is not a tactic favoured by everyone. Some feel that the thief should be uncovered and prosecuted and may even introduce private detectives to catch the culprit. This certainly has a salutary effect in warning off anyone else tempted to steal. Others feel it is bad for the morale of the staff to feel they are under a cloud of suspicion, or that they will be involved in unpleasantness and might be called upon to be a witness. Some feel it is bad for the charity or its reputation to have any suggestion of wrong doing associated with its activities. It is really a question of temperament. Whatever the method to deal with suspected theft it requires a measure of tact, and team building. Giving someone the opportunity to steal is wrong, so build in a security system so losses will be exposed quite quickly.

To prevent staff theft warn everyone that a monitoring system is in place. That is the first line of defence - warning everyone that they are likely to be caught. Secondly, the way in which the shop is run will reinforce, or erode, this belief. A sloppily run shop invites theft. A well run shop creates commitment to the shop's success, and to the charity, and this will make people feel disloyal if they steal.

80% OF LOSSES IN CHARITY SHOPS are thought to be due to theft by staff, paid and voluntary. A small part is due to thefts of cash from the till, or the collecting box; most is by taking donated stock.

Many people would steal in certain contexts, if they can justify it to themselves, and in a charity shop this causes a particular problem. Because the staff may be voluntary they may feel they deserve a little reward for all their hard work. Paid staff may feel they are so poorly paid that they are practically working as volunteers, so they are justified in giving themselves a little extra. The main factor leading to the theft of stock is that it has been donated, it is seen as "thrown away" by the donor, so those sorting the stock do not see picking out the best bits for themselves as the same as stealing. This pre-selection, or 'weeding' as it is known in the trade, is probably the biggest source of loss in charity shops.

Weeding happens largely at the pre-sorting stage, because at that stage the stock is not seen as belonging to anyone. It is simply discarded by the donor, *"thrown out, unwanted goods"*. Once the goods are sorted and hung up on a rail, taking them without paying for them is recognisably nearer to stealing. At this stage the staff may baulk at simply helping themselves to stock but they may not be so circumspect at pricing any item they want at a lower price, thus giving themselves an unauthorised discount.

Both 'weeding' and 'preferential' pricing may be very widespread amongst the staff. It may not even occur to them that what they are doing is wrong, and would be horrified to learn that it was regarded as theft. The charity has to make absolutely clear that once goods are donated they become the property of the charity and that they are given to the charity to convert into cash for its work, not just thrown away.

It is best to have more than one person sorting and pricing. Depending on the availability of staff, it is best to vary the rotas, to prevent collusion.

Have the staff leave their bags in lockers, away from the stock room, so they cannot stuff items into their carrier bags unobserved. In some charity shops staff are not allowed to carry any money on them, on the shop floor. All money has to be put in a locker. This apparently draconian measure, which is standard procedure in high street retailing, is to stop any coins or money that should be put in the till being pocketed, literally.

Lockers should be provided for the benefit of the staff, so they can secure their handbags and coats. Put the lockers in a place where access to them is overseen, and where excessive to-ing and fro-ing would be noticed. Be suspicious of any unexplained visits to the sorting area, because stock which is on a rail waiting to be put out can be stolen, as can stock set aside for a special promotion. If no one is working in the sorting area it should be kept locked.

DONATED STOCK RULES

There should be careful procedures for dealing with all donated stock - which must always be followed. The rules are not guidelines they are rules.

These could be summed up:

- all goods donated to the charity belong to the charity

- those sorting and pricing the goods must not pre-select for their own use at a preferential price

- in no circumstances may the person pricing an item buy it

- all staff purchases must be listed in a staff purchase book

- the amount of stock bought by any one member of staff may be limited

Make sure if stock is taken home to be laundered, or taken to be valued, that it does not disappear. Keep a check. Make sure not just that the same number of items are returned but that they are the same items.

Some charities impose a rule a rule that no item may be bought by a member of staff before it has been displayed in the shop, and offered for sale, for at least two days. This prevents the staff creaming off all the best stock. Staff may think this unfair because they pay for the items, so are customers like anyone else, but it makes the shop less attractive to outsiders, who are only offered second best, and this loses customers, who stop bothering to come in. This should be explained to the staff. Alternatively, allow the staff to purchase anything once it has been priced at double the price if they want to snap it up before it is put out in the shop. (Do not fix the price artificially low to compensate.)

There is always a difficult balance between suggesting to staff, and customers, that you expect them to steal and trusting them. You must make clear that all procedures designed to protect against theft are imposed on everyone, and not specifically targeted against them. Emphasise that these procedures are the norm in the retail trade - telling people Marks and Spencers do the same always seems to inspire confidence, since they have a reputation for honesty and fair dealing. If you imply that it is the norm to steal, then it makes it easier for thief by allowing them to excuse themselves to themselves on the grounds that *"everyone does it"*. It also represents a challenge to some people, who become keen to buck the system, and find it exciting to outwit the management. Putting people on trust can improve their behaviour. A balance needs to be struck.

One needs procedures to promote best practise, to monitor losses and detect them speedily, but to create in the staff a commitment to the shop, and the charity, so that stealing from it becomes unthinkable. It is unlikely that any shop is going to be completely theft free, over a period of time, but that is not an excuse for running them with a siege mentality. The shop has to be open and friendly and the stock accessible, because that is how people shop. There is no virtue in preserving all the stock at the cost of sales.

RULES FOR CASH HANDLING

Theft of cash by staff is less prevalent than 'weeding' of stock. Whilst 'weeding' is not always clearly seen as theft, everyone knows taking money from the till is stealing. There should be precise rules on cash handling. These will not only reduce mistakes, which would inadvertently produce losses for the charity, but they should make it easier to pick up deliberate thefts.

Sales should always be recorded through the till, and all money put in the drawer. Money should never be left on or by the till. If there is no one serving at the till, then the key should be removed, so it is immobilised. Each day the till should be programmed (most tills do this automatically) to show the day's date. All sales will be recorded on the till roll. If the till is opened other than at the time of a sale then the void slip, which comes out of the till like a receipt, should be signed by the person responsible for opening the till, and clipped to the day's till sheet. It is a good idea to have the person working the till sign on and off, on the till roll, so you can see who is responsible. At the end of the day there should be a 'z' reading, which lists the activity at the till, including sales, voids, incorrect ringing ups. The 'z' reading, which gives the day's total take, should be the same as the cash in the till (after accounting for the float). Any discrepancies should be accounted for.

Beware of refunds, they are a wonderful way of taking money from the till and handing it over to brothers, sisters, friends or other accomplices. All refunds should be signed for in a refund book. Ask for some identity, like a giro book or driving licence and note it in the refunds book. Note who is giving the highest number of refunds, and ask yourself if it seems reasonable. Have a policy on refunds, and consider displaying a notice setting out the policy. Customers have a right to return goods that are faulty, and the fault was not clearly marked or indicated at the time of purchase.

RULES FOR CASH HANDLING

- all sales must be recorded through the till
- all money must be put in the till drawer
- never leave money by the till
- the till drawer should be opened only for sales
- the till should be programmed daily
- all 'voids' to be accounted for
- a 'z' reading for each day should be reconciled with cash in the till

You can make clear that whilst recognising the customer's rights under the Sale of Goods Act, 1979, customers must produce proof of purchase, such as a receipt. It is not usual to allow exchanges, unless an assurance has been given to the customer at the time of purchase that goods may be exchanged, for example, if they are for a present.

You can tell a great deal from a till roll. Do not jump to conclusions - there are often simple, but unexpected explanations, to apparently odd behaviour. For example, one sales assistant was responsible for the most enormous number of voids as she used the till in place of a watch to tell her the time! Voids are always something to look for because you have to open the till to take from it. If you were going to steal cash you would probably by-pass the till - simply taking the money and failing to give a receipt. That is why shops have signs on the till enjoining their customers to ask for a receipt. The true amount might not be rung up, so the till registers £4.99, not £9.99 and the thief pockets the £5. If a customer complains then the thief pretends it was a mistake. Customers in a rush who do not wait for a receipt, or to see if the money goes into the till, in effect give the thief a present.

The best safeguard for theft from the till is vigilance. If people are likely to be observed they will usually not try to steal. If you have any reason to suspect theft of cash look carefully at the tell tale signs - the most likely is a drop in the takings at the times when the suspect is working the till. Always compare the performance of a shop over a period of time. You have a pattern of sales, and an expected level of performance. If a shop is failing to reach that level, and you cannot account for it in other ways - for example the staff are rude, there is very little passing trade, the shop's appearance is unattractive - then look at the till rolls. Organise a "ghost" purchase. Send in someone unknown to the staff to make a purchase, and see if it shows up on the till roll, or has the till been by-passed. Get that person to watch the till, surreptitiously, to see if there are any irregularities. It is astounding how flagrant thefts from tills can be. One bemused customer at a café watched the cashier set aside every third sale for themselves, in full view of all the customers. Often one sees a cashier sitting behind permanently open tills, simply using them as cash drawers. Area or regional organisers will make it part of their visit to audit the till - checking cash in the till against the till roll reading. It is best if the visit is unannounced, so the staff do not prepare for it.

The collecting box may be raided by staff. With an average take of £25 a week in some charity shops the collecting box could provide a thief with a steady, supplementary income. Again, monitoring against the performance of other shops is the best way to catch the thief.

Do not think that because the till roll and the day's takings reconcile that is the end of the problem. The money still has to be banked. The stamped receipt, giro form, from the bank should be returned with the till roll 'z' reading and till sheet. Take care to check that the paying in slip is stamped by the bank! There is usually a delay in checking the bank receipts, so you need to check the paying in slip in the interim. It is not unknown for the unstamped slip to be sent into head office, and the money not paid into the bank!

It helps to be aware of the possibilities. Be curious. Notice anything untoward. One can never completely protect oneself against theft, because to do so may so destroy the pleasantness of the shop, and reduce its attractiveness to customers. Some security devices like electronic tagging, cameras or perhaps most effectively extra staff, are too expensive. One has to weigh the cost of the system against the cost of lost stock. For low value items it is generally not worth the investment. But everything should be considered, and periodically re-examined because circumstances might change.

Always investigate any allegations - they may come in the form of anonymous phone calls or letters. Similarly always follow up reports that goods donated to the charity shop have ended up in a car boot sale. There may be a simple honest explanation - for example, someone bought it from the shop and decided to sell it subsequently. It may be that the rag merchant has sold all the bags he was paying you £1 for, for £3 to dealers. In which case you may want to alter your arrangement with the waste merchant, and make it a condition of contract that the goods can only go to waste. People do not realise that over 50% of the goods donated to charity shops are not sold by them through the shops, and it might not be something the charities would want known, as it might lessen the enthusiasm of donors, so take care to avoid what might be an embarrassing situation. Sometimes you will uncover abuse, finding shop staff running a car boot sale business using your donated goods. Do not jump to conclusions. Never accuse anyone before you know for certain, and call in the police if you consider it appropriate. The best defence against theft of any type is vigilance.

6

UNDERSTANDING THE FINANCES

The importance of the figures

The jargon

Working out the profit

Cash flow

Return on capital

Sales per square foot

Working to a budget

The bottom line

THE IMPORTANCE OF THE FIGURES

On the surface it looks foolproof. Donated stock, volunteer labour, VAT concessions, rate reductions - how can a charity shop fail to make a profit. Yet not all charity shops are profitable, particularly when head office support costs are taken into account.

It is important that everyone involved in running a charity shop understands the figures, and the implications for profit and loss. The finances of the shop are not some magic potion cooked up by the book-keeper and auditor, they are an intrinsic part of running the shop; a measure of its success or failure.

THE JARGON

To be able to understand the finances one needs to know some of the technical terms. The person hearing these terms for the first time often feels too embarrassed to ask what they mean, because they feel they should know. But no one is born knowing how to do accounts, and there is no shame in asking, in fact, it is sign of intelligent awareness.

To understand the finances, one has to understand the terms and concepts used, and be sure as to what is being included. The jargon is not always used in the same way, although the new SORPS (Standard of Recommended Practise for Charity Accounting) and Audit rules for company accounts do try to produce standardisation

TURNOVER This means income from all sources. A charity shop's turnover will include money (in the form of cash, cheques, or credit card payments) for sale of goods; donations for the charity's work, which may be handed to an assistant or put in a collecting box; sale of surplus stock to the waste merchant, and any income from sale of stock to dealers or through auction sales. The turnover is all the income of the shop. Turnover is usually measured, and referred to, on an annual basis, for example, someone saying *"the shop turnover is £56,000"* is giving the annual figure. Turnover can be measured weekly, monthly or

---

TURNOVER = the INCOME from ALL SOURCES

- sales of donated goods
- donations
- sales of surplus to waste merchants
- sales at auctions and to dealers

---

quarterly, but usually in these cases the length of time will be given, as in the *"monthly turnover was £4,500"*.

EXPENDITURE encompasses all the costs of running a shop. For convenience, these can be divided into categories. Occupancy costs are all the costs attributed to the premises, including rent, rates, water rates, insurance, heating, lighting and maintenance). Sometimes telephone and cleaning costs will also be ascribed to occupancy, at other times they may be designated separately. The occupancy costs may be described as 'property and depreciation.'

Depreciation is a way of spreading the cost of capital equipment which may last for several years over the period of its working life, rather than heaping all the cost into one year of purchase and 'writing it off'. For example, the shopfittings are paid for in year one. They are expected to last 5 years, so the accountant will take a fifth of the cost and carry it forward over the subsequent years. Or it may be decided that they should be paid for at different rates in each of the years, so 30% is treated as expenditure in year one; 25% in year two and so on.

Staffing Costs includes not only salaries, national insurance and pension provision, but also volunteers' expenses, the costs of recruitment, such as advertisements in the local paper and training costs, where training is provided. The costs of uniform and protective clothing may be included under staff, or it may be separately listed.

EXPENDITURE IS THE SUM OF ALL COSTS INVOLVED IN RUNNING A SHOP. These can be grouped into categories such as:

- occupancy
- staff
- stock costs
- central costs

There are different ways of categorising expenditure. To make meaningful comparisons, one needs to know what is included in each category.

Stock costs (for conventional shops this is often described as **'cost of sales'**). Just because the stock is donated does not mean that it comes absolutely free. There are costs of collection, of appealing for donated goods, of black bags for disposal to the waste merchant, of labels, pricing guns and bags and wrapping materials. If the charity, or more likely its trading subsidiary, buys in goods for re-sale then the cost of these goods would be listed as the cost of sales. Any delivery charge made by the supplier, or other handling charge, must be added to get the true cost of the stock. Since bought in goods have to be treated differently for accounting and VAT purposes it would be usual to list the costs associated with them separately, though they form part of the expenditure of the shop.

'**Running costs**' is sometimes used as a category which encompasses costs such as electricity, till hire, or annual service, telephone, publicity costs, expenses, but it is not always clear what items are in fact included and what apportioned elsewhere. Sometimes this information is included in notes to the accounts. If it is not then it shows an intelligent understanding to ask for clarification.

As well as the direct costs of the shop there well might be **regional and head office costs**. This will be apportioned to each shop. These costs will include supervisory staff, such as area and regional managers, central staff, such as the Finance Officer or National Shops Adviser. Services which the charity is providing for the shops, such as legal advice, promotional material, property maintenance, may all be charged to the individual shops. How the charge is allocated will vary - it may be on the basis of the shop's turnover, so the shop with an annual turnover of £80,000 pays twice as much as one with £40,000 turnover. Or the central costs may simply be allocated on a flat rate to all the shops. Perhaps shops needing the most help, for example, when starting up, are charged more than those shops which took up fewer resources. How charities allocate central costs vary, and the only thing they all have in common is that the individual shops resent this apparent levy, it is more tactful to show the shop results before allocation of central costs, at least to the shops supporters, and make the adjustments in the central accounts, though there is an argument against this, that this encourages people to be unrealistic, and not have an educated and informed view of the finances.

In understanding figures, the first thing any intelligent person will ask is 'what is included' because it is only when you know this that the figures have any meaning, and you consider if they seem reasonable, or too high or too low, compared with other similar operations.

WORKING OUT THE PROFIT

Once the income and the expenditure are known the profitability of each shop can be worked out. It is simply income less expenditure equals net profit. The net profit is the amount left after all the expenses have been taken into account. There is a difference between Receipts and Payments accounts which gives the picture at a specific date, so shows only expenses which have actually been paid for, or payments actually received and Income and Expenditure accounts which take into account monies owed to and by the charity. For example, the Receipts and Payments account shows there is a surplus of £5,000, but an Income and Expenditure account would adjust that figure to give a more accurate view of the true financial situation, to allow for a £400 bill for a new till and a £150 bill for the previous year's window cleaning contract and £600 owed to the charity for sale of a painting by an auctioneer. Receipt and Payment accounts are suitable only for the simplest of organisations, and should only be used by a charity shop as a petty cash system.

The terms 'net profit' and 'gross profit' are often confused with disastrous results. The net profit is the 'bottom line'. It is the real profit after taking off all the expenses. The gross profit is the amount left once the stock is paid for. For example the income (from sales) is £100. The 'cost of sales', i.e.. the cost of stock was £50. The gross profit from which all expenses other than the cost of buying the stock, from which all expenses have to be met, is £50. By knowing the gross profit, you can see if you are allowing yourself sufficient profit margin in which to operate. In conventional retailing if your gross profit falls below 40% you may have problems making a net profit. In charity shops, where the stock is largely donated, the cost of sales (stock) is relatively modest and the gross margin and net margins higher than in conventional shops. This is to be expected.

> **INCOME LESS EXPENDITURE = NET PROFIT**
>
> **Gross profit** is the amount left after paying for the stock net profit is the amount left after paying all expenses.
>
> **Net profit is the real profit.**

CASH FLOW

Cash flow is another term not always understood, though the concept is simple. This describes availability of funds to meet payments. There are many situations in which businesses are in profit, but because, for example, their customers delay in paying invoices, find they do not have enough funds to meet their bills. This problem is not as problematic for charity shops as it is largely a cash business. There is however a seasonal nature to sales - for example, for Oxfam, sales in the shops are concentrated in the last third of the year - with 60% of sales in the shops occurring in the September to December period; and the remaining 40% spread through the other 8 months of the year. You have to have enough working capital to enable you to pay overheads through the year. For example, if you open a shop in February you may not generate sufficient income to meet all costs for the relatively lean months up to September. If you started the shop in August you would be able to accumulate funds to cover the relatively lean months of the year.

Where the charity operates its charity shops directly, rather than through a trading subsidiary, it has rather more flexibility over its cash flow, since it does not have to pass all profits to the parent charity at the end of the financial year, leaving it starved of cash reserves. There is a procedure through which a charity can provide working capital to its trading subsidiary by way of an investment (having considered its viability as a sound investment) but there is an overwhelming duty on the part of the trustees not to provide working capital as an automatic transfer, and the Inland Revenue certainly look askance at the habit of some charities to take the payment of the covenant on one day and hand the money back on the next day as an investment.

RETURN ON CAPITAL

There are many ways of measuring the performance of retail businesses The net profit is the most important. Another useful measure is the return on capital. Since there has to be an investment of resources into the business to set it up and provide working capital, the cost of providing that capital should be considered. Since it is usually the parent charity that provides the capital it is the clear duty of the trustees to ensure that the financial return is at least as good as could be achieved from investing the money in a building society or bank.

It is unrealistic to think that the return on investment will be achieved in the first year, but a schedule should be worked out which shows how the repayment to the charity of the capital and the cost of borrowing at a commercial rate of interest is going to be phased. This should be incorporated into any 'business plan' or budget from the outset, and the ability to meet the borrowing costs taken into account when considering the success or otherwise of the enterprise.

To calculate the return on capital, one simply takes the net profit and divides it into the total amount of capital. For example, the charity has invested £50,000 to develop its shop chain. The net profit in the first year was £20,000. This gives a return on capital of 40%, which would be excellent, much better than a commercial rate of interest. If the investment of £50,000 yields net profits of

CHARITY RANKED BY ROCE	MEAN CAPITAL EMPLOYED	RETURN ON CAPITAL EMPLOYED
Oxfam	11,241,000	163%
Princess Alice Hospice	310,000	131%
Sense	290,049	86%
Save the Children	3,818,000	49%
Children's Society	3,749,125	29%
Barnardo's	12,588,048	22%
British Heart Foundation	4,217,000	20%
Cancer Research Campaign	5,100,000	17%
Helping Hand	1,964,080	10%

Figures from NGO Finance, Annual Survey of Charity Shops 1994. Reproduced by kind permission of the publisher.

£5,000 the rate of return drops to 10%, which would still be acceptable.

Charities achieve different rates of return on capital, ranging from, according to the annual Charity Shops Survey in NGO Finance, 941% to minus 50%. But as the report points out there are enormous differences in calculating these figures, which make comparisons inappropriate. For example, some charities make full provision for property repairs others wait for disaster to strike and charge all repair costs to the year incurred.

The return on capital increases as the shops become established and the original setting up costs are spread over a longer period of trading. Whilst it is hard to compare return on capital between charities, except where they are using similar accounting assumptions, it is interesting to compare the performance of each charity over a period of time, to see if the looked for improvement in the return on capital is being achieved.

SALES PER SQUARE FOOT

A very usual criterion used to judge performance in retailing is the sales per square foot. Thus a shop with a selling area of 1,000 square feet has an annual turnover of £250,000, which gives sales per square foot of £250. The earnings, or sales per square foot, should correlate with the rent level, so a shop in Oxford Street should achieve higher sales per square feet than one in Crewe High Street. For shops selling donated goods the sales per square foot are likely to be much lower than for other retail outlets, but then the cost of stock is much lower.

The measurement of sales per square foot is more useful when used to measure differences between the performance of different shops within a chain, or if possible to compare the performance of apparently similar shops run by other organisations. Since the main costs of running a charity shop are fixed, any increase in turnover means the additional funds go virtually straight into net profit.

WORKING TO A BUDGET

It is possible, and sensible, to draw up a budget for the financial year, to show how the shop is expected to perform financially. The budget is not the Ten Commandments, and may need adjusting in the light of circumstances. Nor is it a weapon to beat people about the head with if they fail to achieve the targets set. It is a way of monitoring expected income and expenditure against actual performance.

> The budget is a way of of monitoring performance against expectation.

To draw up a budget first list the anticipated income. Perhaps this should be done on a monthly or a quarterly basis. Include expected income from all sources - like collecting boxes, sale of goods to customers and rag merchant.

Then list all likely items of expenditure. If you can put these in the months in which payment will fall due you will be able to see if there are any cash flow problems. (Periods in which expenditure exceeds income for which no accumulation funds are available.) Take care to include any expenditure you can possibly imagine. For example, window display equipment, price tags, window cleaning, refuse collection, black plastic bags, Blu-Tack. Allow an amount for sundries. Careless under budgeting will lead to a reduced profit, and an outcome worse than expected.

It is quite hard to draw up a budget with any accuracy. The most reliable figures on which to base ones estimates are the previous year's figures (where there are any). Consider if there have been any material changes which are likely to cause a rise or fall in the figures. For example, will the shop be covered in scaffolding for half the year (so a fall in sales is expected).

Has the rent gone up? Has a water meter been installed so there will be a saving on the water rates? Think about each item and make a judgement as to whether it is likely to rise, fall or stay the same.

Once you have drawn up the budget, consider it. Does it show a net profit? Is it large enough to warrant all the effort. In other words, should you close the shop and send all the volunteers out with collecting boxes? Is it less than you thought. Why? Is it because you have been too cautious both in predicting sales and costs? Could you do anything to increase the profit level? How does your budget compare with other similar shops. Ask shops in your neighbourhood if they will compare notes. If you are part of a national chain the area supervisor will tell you, unasked, how your performance and budget compare with others in the chain.

As the year proceeds measure performance against that predicted in the budget. If expenditure is up, see why, and try to bring it back into line. If sales figures are better, feel pleased, and take the opportunity to thank all the staff.

> Actually, the budget is not as important as reality - it is only a working tool, it does not put money in the till!

The budget is a useful tool if you use it. Too often people draw up a budget, at the insistence of their management, and then never refer to it again. That is a waste of time. Even worse is the scenario where the head office draws up a budget for the shop without any reference to the shop staff, and present it to them as a target which they always fail to achieve. That is very poor management. Those expected to implement the budget should have a say in drawing it up.

Be sceptical of any shop that tells you that it kept to budget - either in achieving income or in its expenditure levels. Those drawing up the budget are not fortune-tellers or soothsayers. They can make an informed guess as to the likely outcomes. If a budget is achieved with one hundred percent accuracy then someone is tampering with the figures. It is important to monitor performance to stay roughly in balance and cut expenditure if income is low and realise the need for higher expenditure if sales are higher than predicted. Look closely at any performance that tallies too closely with the budget!

THE BOTTOM LINE

The most important factor in running a charity shop is to know exactly what it is taking (its income) and what it is costing (its expenditure). It is no good viewing the finances with an optimistic eye - *"Oh we were very busy today, we must be doing well"* and *"every one works for nothing and the stock costs nothing."* Get into the habit of using hard fact.

Only the bankable money is the income. And all costs must be included in the expenditure. Just as with one's household bills the small, unexpected costs can add up very substantially, so too the charity shops expenditure will spread beyond rent, rates and heating. Count everything in to get a true figure.

If you do not take everything into account you will be disappointed and demoralised at the year end results, because of unrealistic expectations. And that is before head office costs are apportioned.

7

HOW PROFITABLE ARE CHARITY SHOPS

How profitable are charity shops

Charities income from their shops

Financial profile of a typical shop

HOW PROFITABLE ARE CHARITY SHOPS

In all charity fund-raising there is a tendency to emulate apparently successful fund-raising ideas of other charities, without a clear understanding as to the true profitability of the operation. Never assume because something looks successful it is. Never assume that *"they wouldn't do it if it wasn't making money"*. Life is full of fools doing foolish things and avoiding reality. The charity sector is not spared them.

Not all charity shops are profitable. They may fail individually, or the overheads of supervising the operation can absorb all the profits.

There is some suggestion that the golden age for charity shops has passed, and the next decade will see decline in an over-sated market. Whilst economic decline in high street retailing has made it easier to find previously prime sites, the changing nature of the town centre and its retailing, reduces the earning capacity of those shops. Late comers to the field may also have to tie up more capital in development of their shops' operation, particularly when they wanted to set up a large operation very quickly, so their profitability, at least in the early years, will be lower.

Not all charities run charity shops. The figures from Charities Aid Foundation's 'Dimensions of the Voluntary Sector 1994' show only 12.5% of the top 200 fund-raising charities had any income from charity shops in 1992/3. In fact, this is an under representation as the CAF figures seem to list the charity shop income of charities which operate their shops through trading companies under trading income.

Figures from 'The 1994 Charity Shop Survey' in NGO Finance identify a further 9 charities listed in the CAF's top 200 fund-raising charities as having charity shops, which would represent 17% of the total. And if one included the further 15 charities identified in the Corporate Intelligence Research Publication's 'Charity Shops in the UK' (1992) whose local branches were operating charity shops (and assuming they were still doing so in 1993) then the proportion of the top 200 fund-raising charities with charity shops would rise to 24.5%.

Charity shops can generate a substantial amount of income for a charity. In 1993, Oxfam's revenue from its charity shops was nearly £19 million, a very substantial part of the charity's total income. No other charities approach the scale of Oxfam's

CHARITY SHOP INCOME OF THE
TOP 200 FUND-RAISING CHARITIES
(CAF 'DIMENSIONS OF THE VOLUNTARY SECTOR 1994')

Charities ranked by total voluntary income 1993		Charity shop income 1993 (or as otherwise stated)
2	Oxfam	18,472,000
4	Save the Children Fund	2,041,000
5	Imperial Cancer Research Fund	6,542,000
6	Cancer Research Campaign	2,491,000
7	Barnardo's	1,501,000
8	Help the Aged	775,000
13	Cancer Relief Macmillan Fund	94,000
14	British Heart Foundation	1,377,000
15	British Red Cross	2,141,000
19	Spastics Society (Scope)	4,856,000
20	Marie Curie Cancer Care	(207,000)
24	Arthritis & Rheumatism Council	16,000
28	Church of England Children's Society	840,000
29	National Children's Home	100,000
33	Multiple Sclerosis Society	59,000
36	Sue Ryder Foundation	2,289,000 (1991)
54	Shelter	178,000
64	Muscular Dystrophy Group	58,000
68	Distressed Gentlefolk's Aid Association	24,000
123	Princess Alice Hospice Trust	591,000
144	British Sailors' Society	62,000
168	Society of Friends of Jewish Refugees	1,691,000
170	Royal Scottish Society for Prevention of Cruelty to Children	30,000
184	East Kent Hospice Project	514,000
197	St. Gemma's Hospice	127,000 (1992)

Note: the income means net profit

1993 figures from 'Dimensions of the Voluntary Sector', 1994 (1st Edition).
Charities Aid Foundation, 1995.

ADDITIONAL CHARITIES LISTED IN 'THE 1994 CHARITY SHOP SURVEY' (NGO FINANCE)[2]

Charities ranked by total voluntary income 1993		Charity Shop Income 1993 (or as otherwise stated)
10	NSPCC	(27,590)
25	People's Dispensary for Sick Animals	313,122
51	UNICEF	19,407
60	National Council of YMCA's	32,103
116	Tenovus	216,596
110	Sense	386,534
111	St. Christopher's Hospice	100,215
126	Ravenswood	36,000 (1994)
164	National Association for Mental Health (MIND)	311,092

Charities not listed as having charity shop income in CAF's 'Dimensions of the Voluntary Sector' but who are included in NGO Finance annual survey on charity shops and who are amongst the top 200 fund-raising charities.

[2] NGO Finance Volume 4 Issue 3 June/July 94. The 1994 Charity Shop Survey, David Phelan.

CHARITIES LISTED IN 'CHARITY SHOPS IN THE UK' (CORPORATE INTELLIGENCE UNIT)[3]

Charities ranked by total voluntary income (no income figures are available)		Number of shops run by local groups 1991
8	RSPCA	50
9	Salvation Army	105
16	Royal National Institute for the Blind	2
47	Age Concern England	210
67	RAF Association	3
71	MENCAP	469
75	Cats Protection League	12
83	Mental Health Foundation	13
86	The Chest, Heart and Stroke Association	1
99	Cystic Fibrosis Trust	8
110	Church Army	1
154	Alzheimer's Disease Society	2
162	Samaritans	min 8
182	Abbeyfield Society	4

Charities with charity shops, not listed in the CAF or NGO Finance surveys. Generally, these charities' shops are operated autonomously by their local branches and thus the national body is normally shown as having no charity shop income.

[3] 'Charity Shops in the UK'. Corporate Intelligence Research Publications Limited 1992.

operation in number of shops, turnover or profit. The Imperial Cancer Research Fund, the next in size, was earning approximately £6.5 million from its charity shops.

FINANCIAL PROFILE OF A TYPICAL CHARITY SHOP

	Weekly figures		Annual figures	
Income	1993	1994	1993	1994
sales of donated goods	819	763	42588	39676
sales of bought in goods	135	96	7020	4992
cash donations	9	9	468	468
total income	£963	£868	£50,076	£45,136
Expenditure				
collection of donated goods6	-	312	-	-
cost of bought in goods	79	-	4108	-
operating costs	308	-	16016	-
property depreciation	207	-	10764	-
head quarter and central costs	-	-	96	-
exceptional items	5	-	260	-
total expenditure	£701	£631	£36,452	£32,812
surplus	£262	£237	£13,624	£12,324

NOTES

1   Presumably this includes sales to waste merchants, which may average £20 per week.

2   The higher the number of volunteers the higher the headquarter costs.

3   Property and depreciation costs varied widely depending on when leases or freeholds were acquired; and how the accounts were drawn up.

4   The turnover would bring the shop into the registration limit for VAT.

Figures taken from NGO Survey 1993 (including unpublished information from the survey). Fuller figures were given in the NGO Report for 1993 than in the 1994 Report.

The amount of turnover of individual charity shops vary enormously, as do the running costs and net profit. NGO Finance annual surveys provide the best source of information, but are inevitably marred by the failure of some of the big players to participate.

FINANCIAL PROFILE OF A TYPICAL CHARITY SHOP

NGO Finance produces figures for a typical charity shop. It shows turnover of £45,136 (1994), down nearly 10% from the previous year. Interestingly, 9% of the income is from cash donations. The costs of running the shop, including overheads, was calculated as £32,812 (happily, 10% down on the previous year). Net profit for the shop was thus £12,324. This profile is very helpful as a realistic view of what the likely turnover is going to be for a charity. Many do much better, many do much worse.

A very significant factor in determining profitability is when the charity acquired premises, either leasehold or freehold. The large swings in retail property price can make a huge difference to the profitability of the shops. The charity which opened shops when the property prices were high has to continue to carry that high cost generally through the period of the lease. Some charities have been more successful at managing their property deals than others, selling leases for premiums, selling freeholds in a rising market, negotiating new leases in a slump, but the job of the charity is not to speculate on property prices, and whilst one lauds shrewd judgement, dealing in property should be seen as a by-product not the purpose of the exercise.

Consider if the use of resources, including the energy of the volunteers could generate more funds. The advantage of a thrift shop is that it provides a relatively steady source of income, that is not earmarked for any project. The shops undoubtedly provide a service to both buyers and donors. They are environmentally desirable. They provide an opportunity for volunteers to help others. But if the bottom line is profit the charity must always ask *'Is this the best use of resources? Could we achieve more for our charity doing something else'.*

15 SIMPLE WAYS TO IMPROVE YOUR SHOP'S PROFITS

- ❏ keep it open longer (costs are fixed)
- ❏ light it better
- ❏ smarten the exterior
- ❏ attract better quality donated stock
- ❏ display it better
- ❏ make the staff thank donors
- ❏ be friendly and welcoming to customers
- ❏ improve staff morale
- ❏ clean and tidy the shop
- ❏ discard unsold stock regularly and ruthlessly
- ❏ get a better price from your rag merchant
- ❏ review pricing policy and adjust as necessary
- ❏ change window displays weekly
- ❏ improve shop layout to lure the customer to the back of the shop
- ❏ give more space to the best selling categories

RESOURCES

PUBLICATIONS

The Inland Revenue: Fund-Raising for Charity: What to look out for on tax. (1994), pamphlet, available from the Inland Revenue.

Kate Sayer: Charities and VAT: a practical guide. (Directory of Social Change, 1992.) £9.95.

The Charity Commission: Fund-Raising and Charities. CC20, (1993).

HM Customs and Excise: Charities and Value Added Tax. (VAT leaflet, 701/1/92.)

Keith Mitchell. Trading by Charities. (Charities Tax Reform Group 1994.) Available from Charities Advisory Trust. Price incl. p+p, £3.95.

Michael Norton (ed): Managing Your Solvency. (Directory of Social Change. 1994). £9.95. This covers the problems of investing in a trading subsidiary and of the new Companies Acts.

Stephen Lloyd: Charities, Trading and the Law. (Charities Advisory Trust.) 1995. £14.95 (available from the Charities Advisory Trust.) A comprehensive guide to the law on charity trading.

Bev Cross: A Practical Guide to Company Law. (Directory of Social Change.) 1994. £7.95. A good basic guide on company law for charities.

NGO Finance (published 6 times a year.) Published by Plaza Publishing Ltd.

Available by subscription only. Publishes an annual survey of charity shops. Copies of June/July 1994 issue, with the 1994 Charity Shop Survey are available from the Charities Advisory Trust (£4 incl p+p.)

W.W. Greathead: Charity Shops: A Guide to their Acquisition, Development and Operation. (Marks and Spencer plc. Baker Street, London.) Available free of charge to charities.

Steve McCurley & Rick Lynch: Essential Volunteer Management. (Directory of Social Change. UK edition. 1994). £14.95

Gill Taylor & Christine Thornton: Managing People. (Directory of Social Change. 1994). £9.95.

Dr Susan Saxon-Harrold (Editor): Dimensions of the Voluntary Sector. (Charities Aid Foundation. 1st edition. 1995). £20.00

Safe Manual Handling (A Scriptographic Booklet), 1988, booklet number 842401D - 9 - 92. Available from Scriptographic Publications Ltd., Butts Road, Alton, Hants, GU34 1ND.

'All Expenses Paid?'
The Volunteer Centre UK
Carriage Row
183 Eversholt Street
London NW1 1BU
Tel: (0171) 388 9888
Fax: (0171) 383 0448

Information on payment of expenses to volunteers.

SUPPLIERS

Suppliers of metal 'clothing banks'

Metal Masters
Unit G - Woodside Industrial
Estate Pedmore Road
Dudley
West Midlands DY2 0RL
Tel: (01384) 76687
fax: (01384) 76687

Suppliers of pricing guns, taggers and labels:-

NOR Systems
Harwich
Essex CO12 4PR
Tel: (01255) 240000
Fax: (01255) 240111

Suppliers of steam presses:-

'Propress'
Davmerry Limited
Propress House
33/35 Battersea Bridge Road
London SW11 3BA
Tel: (0171) 228 8467
Fax: (0171) 924 2549

'Speedy Press'
N.E.C. Building
Tanners Bank
North Shields
Tyne and Wear NE30 1JH
Tel : (0191) 257 7705
Fax: (0191) 257 8640

Suppliers of shop fittings and display material. All
sorts of shop fittings and
display material, including
stands, hangers, tickets, tagging
systems.

Kerr's Displays Ltd
104 Freemens Common Road
Freemens Common
Leicester LE2 7SQ
Tel: (0116) 2543136
Fax: (0116) 2471637

POS Centre
Unit 39 - Wimbledon Stadium
Business Centre
Riverside Road
London SW17 0BA
Tel: (0181) 879 3070
Fax: (0181) 879 7345

Robert May of Holloway Ltd
103 Seven Sisters Road
London N7 7QP
Tel: (0171) 272 5225
Fax: (0171) 272 4313

Information on waste merchants

The Reclamation Association
16 High Street
Brampton
Huntingdon
Cambs PE18 8TU
Tel: (01480) 455249
Fax: (01480) 453680

Health and Safety Regulations (£30 per pack):

HSE Books
PO Box 1999
Sudbury
Suffolk CO10 6FS
Tel: (01787) 881165
Fax: (01787) 313995

Safety standards for products:

The Consumer Safety Unit
Department of Trade and
Industry - Room 302
10-18 Victoria Street
London SW1H ONN

Local Trading Standards
Departments of local
authorities should also be able
to provide information.

In Northern Ireland enquiries
should be made to the
Environmental Health
Department of the local District
Council.

TRAINING

The Distributive Occupational Standards Council
Bedford House
69-79 Fulham High Street
London SW6 3JW
Tel: (0171) 371 7673
Fax: (0171) 371 7742

Sets the standards for National
Vocational Qualifications in
Retailing.

Charities Advisory Trust
Radius Works
Back Lane
Hampstead
London NW3 1HL
Tel: (0181) 794 9835
Fax: (0181) 4313739

Holds an annual conference
and training courses on charity
shops.

Directory of Social Change
24 Stephenson Way
London NW1 2DP
Tel: (0171) 209 4949

Holds courses on
administrative and financial
management for charities.

INDEX

R

S

U

V

W